Employee satisfaction in US banking

Joanna J. Norris

Abstract

This study examined the effect of transformational leadership and collaboration on employees' satisfaction in the United States banking sector. The objectives of this study were to examine the influence of transformational leadership on employee satisfaction in the United States banking sector and to explore the influence of leader-follower collaboration on employee satisfaction in the United States banking sector. The study employed qualitative descriptive research design. The targeted population consists of bank employees that met the inclusion criteria of the study which involve a minimum of 10 years' experience in the banking sector, a minimum of a Bachelor of Science or its equivalent, and an age range of 30 to 45 years. The sample sizes of 25 participants were selected using purposeful sampling technique. Out of the sample, 15 participants were subjected to personal interview while 2 groups of 5 participants each were engaged in focus group discussions via Zoom video teleconferencing. Data collected through interview and focus group discussion were transcribed and coded on MaxQDA software version 12. The coding process, involving axial coding, led to the identification of 17 distinct subthemes which were further consolidated into six overarching themes. Three of these themes corresponded to the first research question, while the remaining three related to the second research question. Employing an inductive thematic analysis approach, the identified themes were examined. The study concluded that transformational leadership has a significant impact on the job satisfaction of banking professionals in the United States. Additionally, it was determined that collaborative interactions between leaders and their followers also play a significant role in influencing employee satisfaction.

Keywords: Transformational Leader, Collaboration, Employees' Satisfaction.

Dedication

I dedicate this dissertation to Almighty God with profound gratitude and reverence for guiding me unwaveringly through the arduous journey that culminates in the successful completion of my doctoral degree. In moments of doubt and despair, it was His boundless grace that provided me with the strength and resilience to persist in the pursuit of knowledge. With each chapter written, every experiment conducted, and each hurdle overcome, I felt His divine presence, an unwavering source of inspiration. I dedicate my dissertation work to my family and friends. My king and seven wonderful and adorable children. Thank you for being there for me throughout the entire doctorate program. A special feeling of gratitude to my late parents, Moses Bobola, Emanuel Babafemi Osidipe, and Elizabeth Eniola Olaseinde Osidipe for your sacrifice and love from the day I was born till you left this world. My sisters Morenikeji Valerie Tillies and Brandy Martins who have supported me throughout the process. Both of you have been my best cheerleaders.

Acknowledgment

I would like to express my deepest gratitude to the individuals who have played a significant role in the successful completion of my dissertation. Your unwavering support, encouragement, and guidance have been instrumental in this academic journey.

First and foremost, I extend my heartfelt appreciation to my husband, Adedayo Abolade, for his unwavering love, patience, and constant encouragement throughout this doctoral endeavor. Your belief in me and your steadfast support have been my pillars of strength.

To my children – Glory, Grace, Gabriel, Gideon, Godfrey, Gabrianne, and Giovanna Abolade – your understanding, patience, and sacrifices did not go unnoticed. Your love and support provided me with the motivation to pursue this academic dream.

I am also immensely grateful to Dr. Felicia Bridgewater, the Director of the program, for her leadership and guidance, which paved the way for this accomplishment. Your vision and dedication to academic excellence have been truly inspiring.

My sincere appreciation also goes to my Chair, Dr. Robert Widner, for his valuable insights, constructive feedback, and steadfast commitment to my academic progress. Your expertise and guidance were indispensable throughout this process.

I would like to acknowledge the members of my committee, whose expertise and feedback enriched the quality of my work. Your valuable contributions were instrumental in refining the content and methodology of my dissertation.

Special gratitude to my academic advisor, Barbara Kelminsky, for her continuous support and mentorship. Your wisdom and guidance have been crucial in shaping the direction of my research. I extend my appreciation to all who contributed in various ways, be it through their knowledge sharing, encouragement, or assistance. Your collective support has played a pivotal role in the successful completion of this dissertation.

This dissertation is not just my accomplishment, but a testament to the collective effort of all who have supported and guided me along the way. Your belief in me and the significance of this research is deeply appreciated, and I am grateful for your unwavering encouragement and support.

List of Tables

Table 1: Demographic Background of the Participants   79

Table 2: Interview/Focus Group Time Average group, and Transcriptions Data   80

Table 3: Analysis of Themes 1, 2 and 3   86

Table 4: Transformational leadership and performance according to Theme 1   87

Table 5: Transformational leadership influences employee loyalty according to Theme 2   92

Table 6: Transformational leadership result to desired outcome according to Theme 3   96

Table 7: Analysis of Themes 4, 5, and 6   100

Table 8: Collaboration and employees' satisfaction according to Theme 4   101

Table 9: Collaboration and best results according to Theme 5   107

Table 10: Collaboration and effective leadership, according to Theme 6   110

Table of Contents

Table of Contents vii

Chapter 1: Introduction to the Study 1

Purpose of the Study 3
Statement of Problem 5
Definition of Terms 7
Theoretical Framework 8
Fielder's Contingency Theory 8
Great Man Theory 10
Research Questions 12
Scope of the Study 13
Significance of the Study 14
Discussion of Assumptions 16
Limitations of the Study 17
Delimitations of the study 19
Summary 20

Chapter 2: Literature Review 22

Introduction 22
Conceptual Framework 22
Definition of Leadership 23
Various Types of Leadership 23
Leadership Skills 28
The Concept of Transformational Leadership 28
Components of Transformational Leadership 29
    Idealized Influence 30
    Inspirational Motivation 32
    Intellectual Stimulation 33
    Individualized Consideration 34

Transformational Leadership Process.. 35

Antecedents of Transformational Leadership.. 36

Relationship between transformational leadership and Employees' Satisfaction 38

Importance of Job Satisfaction.. 39

Measurement of Job Satisfaction 40

The Effect of Transformational Leadership on Employees' Satisfaction in the United States Banking Sector 42

Transformational Leadership and Employees' Performance.. 43

The Effect of Collaboration between Leaders and Followers on Employees' Satisfaction 44

Conditions under which Transformational Leadership becomes Successful in relation to Employees' Satisfaction.. 46

Empirical Review... 47
    Review of Previous Literature on Transformational Leadership 47

Summary.. 50

Chapter 3: Methodology.. 52

Introduction.. 52

Research Methodology 52

Research Design... 54

Population and Sample... 56

Data Sources 61

Research Procedures.. 63

Project Data Analysis... 67

Protection of Human Rights... 69

Delimitations and Limitations.. 71

Assumptions, Risks and Biases.. 72

Trustworthiness of the Research.. 74

Significance of the Study 75

Summary.. 77

Chapter 4: Data Analysis and Results 79

Introduction 79

Data Analysis 81
    Preparation of Raw Data 81

Descriptive Findings 83

Data Analysis Procedures 85

Results 89

Results for Supporting Research Question 1 90
    Theme 1: Transformational Leadership Enhances Performance in Relation to Job Satisfaction 92
    Theme 2: Transformational Leadership Influences Employee Loyalty 97
    Theme 3: Transformational Leadership Result to Desired Outcome 101

Results for Supporting Research Question 2 104
    Theme 4: Collaboration and Employees' Satisfaction 106
    Theme 5: Collaboration and Best Results in Terms of Employee Satisfaction .. 111
    Theme 6: Collaboration and Effective Leadership 114

Summary 118

Conclusion 121

Chapter 5: Summary, Conclusions, and Recommendations 124

Introduction and Summary of Study 124

Summary of Findings and Conclusion 125

Limitations of the study 131

Suggestions for Future Research 133

Chapter 1: Introduction to the Study

Leadership is a learning process premised on increased knowledge to deal with dynamism in the business environment and continuous practice (Effiyanti et al., 2021). A good leader usually expects increased organizational performance (Effiyanti et al., 2021). According to Effiyanti et al. (2021), leadership is a tool employed by leaders to influence individuals, ensuring comprehension of directives and agreement on objectives and strategies for attaining a shared goal. An evaluation of diverse literature on organizational behavior states that the leadership within an organization significantly influences organizational behavior (Stewart et al., 2019). An analysis of modern management practices reveals that many emphases are placed on the need to encourage good leadership and organizational behavior (Stewart et al., 2019).

The need for good leadership and organizational behavior is influenced by the fact that organizations are now unique from earlier times. Unlike when little consideration was given to organizational behavior because stakeholders such as staff members had little say in organizational practices, modern organizational practices require accountability in diverse aspects (Stewart et al., 2019). Sound leadership and organizational behavior have also been noted to positively impact innovation and retain the best talent, two critical factors enhancing organizational success (Stewart et al., 2019).

Transformational leadership has gained prominence in leadership philosophy during the last two decades. It is not surprising that the existing evolution in leadership theory and practice has gained the interest of both researchers and practitioners (Khanetal, 2020). Transformational leadership is a type of leadership that emphasizes the achievement of changes in values, beliefs, attitudes, behaviors, emotions, and subordinates' needs to achieve better results in the future (Effiyanti et al., 2021). Transformational leaders who focus on assisting their followers to achieve a high level of success drive them to be more inspired and committed, which enhances the followers to align their individual goals with the organizational goal (Torlak & Kuzey, 2018).

Also, transformational leadership is significant to an organization because it relates to the activities that exist within an organization (Hasmin & Stem, 2019). This leadership style is characterized by behaviors that inspire subordinates to achieve satisfactory performance. Leaders are expected to pay attention to the working environment so that employees can consistently carry out their duties (Hasmin & Stem, 2019). According to Kotamena et al. (2020), it was posited that transformational leadership involves the capacity of a leader to motivate their followers to surpass anticipated levels of performance and attain superior outcomes. The ideal influence where the subordinates believe in the leader and are emotionally attached to the leader improves employees' satisfaction (Purwanto et al., 2020).

Job satisfaction is regarded as an aspect that has recently gained prominence (Jameel & Ahmad, 2019). Numerous studies emphasize that job satisfaction explains employees' feelings and attitudes about the assortment of intrinsic and extrinsic job satisfaction. Job satisfaction describes employees' contentment with their jobs in the workplace (Jameel & Ahmad, 2019). Presently, there is a limited study conducted on the effect of transformational leadership on employees' satisfaction in the United States. The review of relevant literature revealed numerous relationships between transformational leadership and employee satisfaction. Khan et al. (2020) investigated the effects of transformational leadership on employees' job satisfaction in the United Arab Emirates. According to the study findings, the five characteristics of transformational leadership and total transformational leadership have a considerable positive impact on employee satisfaction. Jameel and Ahmad (2019) examined the effect of transformational leadership on job satisfaction among academic staff at Cihan University-Erbil using responses from 137 respondents. The study's evidence revealed significant positive influence of transformational leadership on the academic staff of Cihan University. In research by Hasmin and Stiem (2019), they examined the effect of transformational leadership on employees' satisfaction and performance in Indonesia. According to the study's findings, transformational leadership has a direct impact on staff performance and an indirect impact on employee satisfaction.

Arumugan et al. (2019) investigated the effect of transformational and transactional leadership styles on employees' satisfaction in conglomerate companies. The research evidence suggested that transformational and transactional leadership styles significantly correlate to employee satisfaction. Odeh (2020) also examined the effect of transformational leadership on employees' innovativeness and job satisfaction in Kuwait's private sector. The findings provided evidence that a notable and positive correlation exists between transformational leadership and employee satisfaction. Andika et al. (2020) also evaluated the effect of transformational leadership and job satisfaction on employees' performance through work motivation in Indonesia. The results of the findings showed that transformational leadership and job satisfaction have significant positive effects on employees' performance. This study aimed to address the literature gap by assessing the impact of transformational leadership on employee satisfaction in the United States banking sector. In previous research within the banking sector, Singh (2019) found that transformational leadership was ineffective in influencing employee satisfaction.

Purpose of the Study

The purpose of this qualitative descriptive study was to investigate the influence of transformational leadership on employees' satisfaction and the influence of collaborations between the leaders and followers on employees' job satisfaction in the United States banking sector. The study's population consists of all employees working in the United States banking sector. For the purposes of this study, sample sizes of 25 participants were picked using the purposeful sampling technique. Out of this sample size, 15 respondents were subjected to a personal interview, 10 other respondents were engaged in focus group discussions, and each focus group comprised five participants. Each focus group had five participants and the participants for the focus group discussions were not the same with the participants for interview. The following precise objectives were met during this research paper: The study looked at the influence of transformational leadership on employee satisfaction in the banking industry in the United States. The qualitative descriptive research design was used in this study. The specific objectives of this research were as follows:

1. To examine the influence of transformational leadership on employee satisfaction in the United States banking sector. Previous studies by Malik et al. (2017) have indicated that transformational leaders create a supportive and empowering environment for their followers, leading to higher levels of satisfaction.

2. To explore the influence of leader-follower collaboration on employee satisfaction in the United States banking sector. According to Chen et al. (2022), transformational leadership includes the element of leadership charisma, where leaders collaborate with their followers to foster an employee-centered climate. This type of climate promotes positive attitudes and enhances workplace satisfaction.

Statement of Problem

The United States banking sector plays a pivotal role in the nation's economy, and the satisfaction and engagement of its employees are essential for sustained growth and success. Transformational leadership, characterized by inspirational motivation, individualized consideration, intellectual stimulation, and idealized influence, has been widely recognized as a leadership style that can significantly impact organizational outcomes, including employee satisfaction. However, despite the theoretical and practical significance of transformational leadership, there exists a gap in the current literature regarding its specific influence on employees' satisfaction within the context of the United States banking sector.

Given the competition that businesses face in a bid to make profits and remain in business, the most crucial task for any leader is to get the best out of employees, which helps organizations remain operationally and financially sustainable (Akparep & Mogre, 2019). The business environment constantly undergoes significant transformations because of globalization (Akparep & Mogre, 2019). Many leaders have discovered that their roles in the workplace are becoming more complex due to dynamism in the business environments (Akparep & Mogre, 2019).

Leadership is a management function that drives a group towards achieving a common goal. It is one of the critical determinants of employee satisfaction (Akparep & Mogre, 2019). A leader only accomplishes success with the active support of subordinates (Akparep & Mogre, 2019). Collaboration between leaders and followers is essential for achieving high organizational performance through employee satisfaction. Thus, leaders' role in enhancing employee satisfaction cannot be over-emphasized. Since the leadership style practiced by an organization influences the success or failure of its operations, thus, the need to investigate the effect of transformational leadership on employee satisfaction arises.

Transformational leadership is chosen in this study because it is a leadership model that seems promising in terms of managing dynamism in organizations since it is a leadership style that has demonstrated a positive effect on both employees' satisfaction and organizational success. El., Toufaili (2017) asserts that transformational leadership is a key element that assures the success of an organization through the generation of greater involvement in the work of subordinates. Kilic and Uludag (2021) also posit that transformational leadership emphasizes subordinates' values, considerations, and emotions to achieve organizational success. There is a need to investigate the conditions under which transformational leadership becomes successful in relation to employees' satisfaction and willingness to serve (Suwanto et al., 2022). Also, examining the perspectives of transformational leadership in enhancing organizational performance is imperative.

Furthermore, it is important to study leadership and organizational behavior to examine how employees behave and perform in the workplace and how they are directed to improve their satisfaction. In this study, the literature gap is filled by investigating the effect of transformational leadership on employees' satisfaction in the banking sector of the United States economy. Banks continue encountering operational challenges due to global economic instability (Yunita et al., 2023). While transformational leadership is often touted as an effective leadership style, there is a dearth of empirical studies that examine its direct impact on employees' satisfaction levels within United States. banks. This research investigated the impact of transformational leadership on employees' satisfaction in the United States banking sector despite the volatile macroeconomic conditions faced by banks.

Definition of Terms

The key terms used in this study are defined as follows:

i. **Employee Innovativeness:** This refers to engagement in innovative work behaviors, including the innovative process behaviors (Satyendra, 2019).

ii. **Employee Performance:** It is defined as employees' outcomes that meet the job requirements (Top et al., 2020). This phenomenon can be comprehended by examining the achievements of coworkers within the professional environment (Top et al., 2020).

iii. **Employee Satisfaction:** It refers to an expression of the pleasure and inner peace experienced by employees in general (Chandrasekara, 2020).

iv. **Ethical behavior:** This consists of transparent behavior, attention to stakeholders' interests, responsibility, loyalty, and compliance with relevant regulations (Widyanti et al., 2020).

v. **Globalization:** This is defined as the growing interdependence of the world economies, cultures, and populations precipitated by cross-border trade in goods and services, the flow of investment, technology, people, and information (Peterson Institute for International Economics, 2021).

vi. **Organizational Behavior:** refers to people's thoughts, feelings, emotions, and actions in a work environment. Organizational behavior is defined as the study of human behavior in a workplace, the interface between human behavior, the organizational context, and the organization itself (Saravanakumar, 2019).

vii. **Organizational goal:** This is the target point or result that a firm attempts to attain in a future determinable time. Also, it is a desired situation that an organization attempts to realize (Santosh, 2021).

viii. **Transformational leader:** It is a leader who is energetic, enthusiastic, and passionate and focuses on helping his/her followers to succeed (Cherry, 2020).

ix. **Transformational Leadership:** A leadership style in which the leader follows synergy, mutual respect, communication, and delegation to achieve individual and organizational goals (Khan et al., 2020).

x. **Vision:** This is a statement that defines the long-run achievement of a firm. It sets a defined guideline for the planning and execution of corporate-level strategies (CFI, 2021).

Theoretical Framework

There are numerous schools of thought that offer explanations on leadership and the requirements of a good leader. This study utilizes two leadership theories applicable to many organizations: " Fielder's Contingency Theory" and "Great Man Theory."

Fielder's Contingency Theory

Fielder's Contingency Theory, developed by Fred Fiedler in the 1960s, proposes that effective leadership depends on the match between the leader's style and the situational context (Kanji et al., 2023). The theory proposes that a leader's style can be either task-oriented or relationship-oriented, and the effectiveness of the leadership style depends on three key situational factors: leader-member relations, task structure, and positional power (Simha, 2022). In the banking sector, these situational factors can vary widely. For instance, in a large national bank, the leader-member relationship may be less personalized due to the size of the organization, while in a community bank, it might be more personalized. Task structure can differ based on the complexity of financial products and services offered. Position power may vary depending on the organizational hierarchy.

The theory also suggests that the effectiveness of a leader's style has implications for various outcomes, including employee satisfaction. Transformational leadership is often associated with higher job satisfaction due to its focus on inspiring and engaging employees (Vinh et al.,2022). Understanding the contingency factors that influence the effectiveness of transformational leadership in the banking sector can have practical implications. Organizations can use this knowledge to tailor leadership development programs and training to ensure that leaders are equipped to adapt their styles to the specific needs of their teams and situations.

The theory is called contingency theory because it asserts that a leader's effectiveness depends on how well his/her approach fits into the context (Shala et al., 2021). This theory maintains that how a leader leads in one environment differs from how another leads in another environment. Fielder's contingency theory suggests that the effectiveness of a leader's style depends on situational factors. In collaborative environments, where teamwork and open communication are crucial, a transformational leadership style tends to be more effective.

Transformational leaders inspire collaboration by fostering a shared vision, encouraging creativity, and creating a positive and supportive team culture. The theory revealed that employees' satisfaction in one bank differs from another bank depending on the leadership style practiced by the bank. The essence of Fielder's theory is that a leader's effectiveness depends on a combination of his/her managerial style and the favored situation (Shala et al., 2021). The theory was developed by an Austrian known as Fred Fielder. Fielder's contingency theory is arguably the best researched example, in terms of quantity of empirical tests of the integrative approach (Souza, 2020). It considers the joint effects of trait variables and the nature of the situation in which the leaders find themselves.

Fielder argued that the approach of effective leadership depends on the contingencies of the situation, the demanding nature of the task and how secure they are (Shala et al., 2021). The contingency theory emphasizes the contingent relationship of leadership performance based on a framework of leadership style scale known as the "Least Preferred Co-worker Scale (LPC)." This relationship is moderated by a favoritism dimension, which refers to the degree to which the leadership situation allows the leader to control and influence their group's behavior (Shala et al., 2021). Fielder's contingency theory further states that leaders with low LPC scores work better in favorable and relatively unfavorable situations with high LPC scores. Fielder uses the distinction between task-oriented leadership and relationship-oriented leadership style, relating these leadership styles with different types of situation in order to determine the contingencies that make the two styles effective (Chaturved, 2017).

Great Man Theory

The Trait Theory is another name for the Great Man Theory of Leadership (Benmira & Agboola, 2020). According to this notion, good leaders are born rather than manufactured or trained. In other words, it is believed that only a few individuals possess the unique characteristics of effective leaders and attain greatness by divine design (Benmira & Agboola, 2020). It was argued that these few individuals were natural-born leaders with innate leadership characteristics, enabling them to lead individuals successfully.

This makes them possess the innate traits and skills required to make them great. The Great Man Theory emphasizes that leaders deserve to be in their best position due to their unique qualities. The collaboration between a leader that possesses innate skills and traits, and the followers will enhance employees' satisfaction. While the Great Man Theory is generally considered outdated, some organizations may still rely on trait-based criteria when selecting leaders, including in the banking sector.

Understanding how certain traits or qualities are perceived as valuable in leadership within this sector can provide insights into leadership development and selection practices.

Transformational leadership emphasizes the importance of leaders inspiring and motivating their employees. While the Great Man Theory focuses on inherent traits, this study explored how transformational leaders within the banking sector may possess or develop specific traits that align with the transformational leadership style, such as charisma, adaptability, and communication skills.

    The Great Man theory was introduced as the earliest theory of leadership. This theory posits that great leaders are innate, and the theory was standard in the 19th and early 20th centuries (Madanchian et al., 2016). The Great Man theory views great leaders as heroic, mythic and that they possess exceptional leadership traits. The theory tried to explain leadership in the view of inheritance, which was premised on the fact that the leader is genetically able to possess higher qualities that distinguish him from his followers (Madanchian et al., 2016). Research scholars have investigated ancient leaders such as Napoleon, Alexander the Great, and Genghis Khan (Hunt & Fedynich, 2018). Their leadership assumed a certain born ability to lead. A leader should emulate historical leaders to become great. There is a lot of criticism of Great Man Theory on the proposition that leaders are either born or not. This theory lacks empirical data to prove the validity of this assumption (Hunt & Fedynich, 2018).

Research Questions

This research was conducted because leadership is a vital component of the management process that helps direct a firm's resources to improve its efficiency and achieve its set goals (Akparepetal, 2019). This study provided answers to the following research questions:

RQ1: How do bank employees describe the influence of transformational leadership on their job satisfaction?

Transformational leaders improve employees' performance by achieving organizational goals and thus implement a reward system that enhances employees' satisfaction (Abouraia & Othman, 2017). The idea of transformational leadership is premised on the fact that transformational leaders encourage followers to get the organization's desired outcome through employee satisfaction (Malik et al., 2017). To promote employee satisfaction, transformational leaders create a new and original management understanding for the followers based on their special features (Malik et al., 2017).

Transformational leadership encourages employees' satisfaction, which enables them to perform tasks effectively, thereby increasing their performance (Khanetal., 2020). This question was chosen because it explains how transformational leadership influences employees' satisfaction. The question is connected to the purpose of the study because it examines how transformational leaders inspire their followers to have a shared vision of set goals, thereby enhancing employees' satisfaction (Khan et al., 2020).

RQ2: How do bank employees describe the influence of collaborations between leaders and followers on employee satisfaction? It is a situation whereby both the leader and the followers assist each other at work (Taylor & Hill, 2017). Effective collaboration coupled with effective leadership enhances employees' satisfaction (Taylor & Hill, 2017). This question was chosen because it helps understand how the collaborations between leaders and followers affect employee satisfaction. This question is related to the purpose of the study by considering how leaders concentrate more on individual requirements and build a strong collaboration with their followers with a view to enhancing employees' satisfaction.

Scope of the Study

This qualitative descriptive study explored the impact of transformational leadership on employees' satisfaction in the United States banking sector and the influence of collaboration between the leaders and followers on employees' satisfaction. The scope of the study covers employees of banks listed on the New York Stock Exchange. The study's geographical boundaries are confined to the United States, with a specific emphasis on the country's banking industry. The primary concentration is directed towards this sector, which encompasses a diverse range of financial institutions, including national banks, regional banks, community banks, credit unions, and other entities operating within the United States.

The methodological scope of the study is firmly rooted in qualitative research analysis, employing a combination of interviews as the primary data collection technique. Qualitative research analysis is chosen as the overarching methodological framework due to its suitability for exploring the nuanced aspects of the research topic. Interviews, a qualitative data collection technique, was selected as the principal means of gathering rich and in-depth insights from participants, allowing for a comprehensive exploration of the influence of transformational leadership on employee satisfaction in the United States banking sector. This approach enables the study to delve deeply into the perspectives, experiences, and perceptions of individuals within this context, contributing to a holistic understanding of the subject matter. The research also considered two leadership theories and their application to the business world: Fielder's Contingency Theory and Great Man Theory.

Significance of the Study

This study addresses a notable gap in the existing literature. While transformational leadership has been extensively studied in various contexts, there is a lack of empirical research specifically examining its influence on employee satisfaction within the United States banking sector. This gap suggests that there is a need for a focused investigation into the relationship between transformational leadership and employee satisfaction in this specific industry. The study aligns with and contributes to the current literature on leadership and employee satisfaction. It builds upon the existing body of knowledge by applying the principles of transformational leadership theory to the unique context of the United States banking sector. By doing so, it bridges the gap between leadership theory and the practical challenges and dynamics faced by organizations within this industry.

The theoretical foundation of this study is rooted in Fielder's Contingency Theory. This theory posits that leaders who inspire and motivate their followers can have a significant impact on employee satisfaction, engagement, and organizational performance. By grounding this research in this theory, it provided a solid framework for understanding how specific leadership behaviors may influence employee satisfaction levels in United States banks.

Employees' satisfaction can be achieved if organizations promote transformational leadership (Chai et al., 2017). Thus, raising transformational leaders will enable the followers to derive the positive effect of transformational leadership (Chai et al., 2017). According to Steinmann et al., (2018), transformational leadership impacts employees' performance through the transformation of the followers who transcend beyond self-interests for the sake of organizational interest (Steinmann et al., 2018).

This research is also essential because transformational leaders commit themselves to selfless ideals to align their values with that of their followers and the organization (Luk & Lazoo, 2020). This study also considers the main components of transformational leadership that enhances employee satisfaction-idealized influence, inspirational motivation, intellectual stimulation, and individualized consideration. This research is very useful in the banking sector of the United States economy because it serves as a road map for the analysis of the effect of transformational leadership on employee satisfaction in the banking sector of the United States economy. The banking sector of the United States economy was considered because there is a limited study that focuses on the effect of transformational leadership on employee satisfaction in the United States banking sector. Thus, this research filled the gap identified from the review of the literature.

Transformational leadership is suggested to be a key driver for business success and a better workplace experience since the interactions between the transformational leader and the followers significantly impact employees' satisfaction and, ultimately, the performance of the organization at large (Li et al., 2019). This research differs from other studies on the effect of transformational leadership on employee satisfaction because of its emphasis on the United States banking sector based on a qualitative study. Transformational leadership can be understood as creating a vision and delivering a sense of belonging to employees (Tse, 2008). This study was relevant at both micro and macro levels, and as such, it acted as a valuable guide for banks in the United States economy as well as other sectors of the United States economy. Job satisfaction is one of the most complicated areas bank managers face today when it comes to managing their employees (Abdolshah et al., 2018).

This study investigated the influence of transformational leadership and collaboration on employees' satisfaction in the United States banking sector. The study's findings are useful for academics and future researchers who may want to research the effect of transformational leadership on employee satisfaction. The recommendations made in this study are beneficial to the parties mentioned above by providing empirical evidence to individuals, government entities, and corporate bodies who may want to conduct further research on the research area.

Discussion of Assumptions

The topic you're proposing involves investigating the impact of transformational leadership and collaboration on employee satisfaction and job satisfaction in the United States banking sector. Conducting a research on the impact of transformational leadership and collaboration on employee satisfaction and job satisfaction in the United States banking sector using a qualitative descriptive approach can provide valuable insights into the experiences and perceptions of employees. The assumptions pre-empted for this study are:

i. Transformational leadership enhances employees' satisfaction: One assumption is that transformational leadership, characterized by visionary leadership, inspiration, and individualized consideration, positively affects employee satisfaction. This assumption aligns with existing research that suggests transformational leaders can motivate employees to achieve beyond their expectations and foster a sense of personal growth and purpose (Andriani et al., 2018). In the banking sector, transformational leaders might create a more engaging work environment, which could contribute to higher job satisfaction.

ii. Collaboration contributes to job satisfaction: Another assumption is that collaboration among employees fosters job satisfaction. Collaboration encourages open communication, idea sharing, and mutual support (Köhler et al., 2022). In the banking sector, collaboration can lead to efficient problem-solving, improved customer service, and a sense of being part of a cohesive team. Higher levels of collaboration might lead to increased job satisfaction as employees feel more valued and connected to their peers.

Limitations of the Study

The potential limitations that could be associated with study on the impact of transformational leadership and collaboration on employee and job satisfaction in the United States banking sector are:

i. Sampling Bias: The study's findings is limited by the sample's representativeness. When the sample consists of employees from only a few specific banks or regions, it creates a situation where the results might not accurately reflect the diverse and multifaceted nature of the entire United States banking sector. The limited scope of the sample could lead to an overemphasis on certain organizational cultures, leadership styles, or collaboration dynamics, potentially skewing the conclusions drawn from the study. To mitigate the impact of sampling bias, the researcher considered purposive sampling technique using the exclusion and inclusion criteria and ensured broader range for participants.

ii. Subjective Perceptions: Employee satisfaction and job satisfaction are complex concepts that go beyond objective measures (Paliga et al., 2022). They encapsulate a range of personal feelings, attitudes, and evaluations regarding various aspects of work environment, including relationships with colleagues, tasks, compensation, and opportunities for growth. Because these constructs are intimately tied to individuals' personal experiences and expectations, they are prone to a multitude of subjective influences. Participants may hold unique viewpoints and interpretations of what constitutes satisfaction. Their individual perceptions, influenced by factors such as personal values, background, past experiences, and current circumstances, can shape how they assess their own satisfaction levels. This diversity of perspectives is a natural and inherent aspect of the human experience, and it introduces the possibility that different participants might interpret and rate their satisfaction differently, affecting the overall validity of the results. To minimize the impact of subjective perceptions on this study, the researcher provided clear definitions of employee satisfaction and job satisfaction to avoid ambiguity and facilitate consistent responses.

iii. Social Desirability Bias: Social Desirability Bias is a psychological phenomenon that can significantly impact research. This bias arises when participants alter their responses to align with what they perceive as socially desirable or acceptable, rather than providing genuine and candid responses (Smallpage et al., 2023). This bias could introduce an overestimation of positive relationships between transformational leadership, collaboration, and satisfaction, distorting the accuracy of your findings. To mitigate the impact of social desirability bias, the researcher assured participants that their responses will remain anonymous and confidential, encouraging them to share their honest opinions without fear of judgment.

iv. Self-Report Bias: Data collected through interviews, surveys, or focus groups might be subject to self-report bias, as participants might not accurately recall or report their experiences or feelings. This bias arises from the fact that individuals might not always accurately recall or honestly report their experiences, emotions, or perceptions which can potentially introduce inaccuracies into the collected data, leading to less reliable findings (Gomes et al., 2022). To address self-report bias the researcher designed the interview questions with clarity and precision to minimize the potential for misinterpretation. Each question was further explained to participants for clear understanding.

v. Ethical Concerns: Ethical considerations related to privacy, anonymity, and informed consent might impact the willingness of participants to share their experiences candidly. To address ethical concern, the researcher using the consent form, clearly explained the process on how participants' data will be collected, stored, and used.

Delimitations of the study

This study takes into account the following delimitations.

i. Geographical Scope: The geographical scope of this study is confined to the realm of the United States banking sector. The research focuses exclusively on this specific industry within the geographical boundaries of the United States. Consequently, the study does not encompass any other sectors or international banking environments outside the United States. By confining the investigation to this particular geographic context, the study aims to delve deeply into the dynamics, challenges, and relationships within the United States banking sector, providing a comprehensive understanding of the subject matter within this localized scope.

ii. Leadership style: The research focused with exclusivity on the examination of transformational leadership as the central and primary leadership style of interest. By honing in solely on transformational leadership, the research design aimed to facilitate a comprehensive and thorough investigation into the specific impacts and implications associated with this particular leadership style. This focused exploration permitted the research to avoid potential confounding effects that might arise when multiple leadership styles are considered simultaneously. By isolating transformational leadership, the study aimed to provide a comprehensive and in-depth analysis of its direct contributions to the subject matter. As a result, the research intended to contribute valuable insights into the specific mechanisms by which transformational leadership intersects with collaboration, influencing the satisfaction of employees and the broader organizational context within the United States banking sector.

iii. Research approach: The research approach employed for this study centered around the qualitative methodology. Qualitative research involves a comprehensive exploration and interpretation of the underlying meanings, nuances, and contexts that shape the phenomenon under investigation. In this study, the qualitative approach was chosen to capture the rich and intricate insights into the impact of transformational leadership and collaboration on employee satisfaction and job satisfaction within the United States banking sector.

Summary

This study shows how adopting the transformational leadership style increases employee satisfaction. A questionnaire was used to determine the leadership style adopted by the banks, and purposefully sampled participants (employees) were selected from banks that indicate a transformational leadership approach is being used. The research contributes to the existing body of knowledge on the effect of transformational leadership on employee satisfaction in the United States banking sector. This was attained through the provision of robust theoretical and empirical evidence on how transformational leadership impacts employees' satisfaction in the United States banking sector. This was achieved by analyzing the views of the 25 respondents chosen as the sample size. Of the 25 respondents, 15 were interviewed one-on-one, while 10 engaged in focus group discussions.

The research also provides valuable support for considering transformational leadership as an integral factor that improves employee satisfaction. There is substantial research evidence to show a significant positive relationship between transformational leadership and employee satisfaction. Using a qualitative research approach, this study added to the existing literature by providing both theoretical and empirical evidence on the effect of transformational leadership on employee satisfaction in the United States banking sector.

Chapter 2: Literature Review

Introduction

In this section of the research paper, an extensive and comprehensive review of the existing literature pertaining to the influence of transformational leadership on employees' satisfaction was conducted. This literature review aimed to provide a thorough understanding of the subject by synthesizing and analyzing a diverse array of studies, theories, and empirical evidence related to the topic. The literature review encompassed a broad spectrum of sources, including scholarly articles, academic papers, books, and relevant reports. By examining a wide range of literature, the review aimed to capture the richness and complexity of the relationship between transformational leadership and employee satisfaction, while also identifying key gaps in the existing research. Furthermore, the theoretical underpinnings that serve as the foundation for the development of the research framework were explored in depth. These theoretical foundations are critical in shaping the study's conceptual framework and guiding the research design and methodology. The discussion delved into various relevant theories, with a primary focus on transformational leadership theory, as it is the central theoretical framework for the study. Transformational leadership theory posits that leaders who inspire and motivate their followers can lead to higher levels of employee satisfaction, engagement, and organizational performance. By elucidating the key principles and concepts of this theory, the section provided a clear and robust theoretical basis upon which the subsequent research was built.

Conceptual Framework

Definition of Leadership

Leadership is a position of authority where one person has the ability to influence or change the values, beliefs, behaviors, and attitudes of other people (Hao & Yazdanifard, 2015). An individual with strong leadership ability will be a role model to their followers (Hao & Yazdanifard, 2015). Leadership can also be defined as a social influence process where the leader determines the organizational objectives and encourage behaviors in pursuit of these objectives (Allrowward et al., 2017). Altamony et al. (2016) also defined leadership as the ability to influence, motivate and enable others to contribute to the success and effectiveness of their organization. Kesting et al. (2016) defined leadership as a process by which an individual is motivated or influenced by a superior officer to achieve a set goal. It is also the process by which an individual influences other in order to attain group or organizational goals (Malik & Azmat, 2019). Managers exercise control, emphasize rationality, expect employees to operate effectively, and do not partake in risk-taking activities (Altamonyetal.,2016).On the other hand, leaders make practical efforts to perform tasks, have personal attributes toward achieving goals, and perform risk-taking activities (Altamony et al., 2016).

Various Types of Leadership

Leadership is a multi-dimensional phenomenon that involves a type of responsibility aimed at achieving particular ends by applying the available resources and ensuring a cohesive and coherent organization in the process (Dwibedi,2016). The concept of leadership style pertains to the behavioral tendencies exhibited by a leader, encompassing various approaches such as visionary, collaborative, coaching, and consensus-building (Gadirajurrettetal.,2018). Different leadership styles exist, but not every style is right for everyone (Gadirajurrett et al.,

2018). The culture and goals of an organization determine the most suitable leadership style (Gadirajurrett et al., 2018). Developing an effective leadership style is instrumental in cultivating the qualities necessary to excel as a proficient leader (Gadirajurrett et al., 2018). There are numerous types of leadership styles in practice. These include charismatic leadership, autocratic leadership, transactional leadership, democratic leadership, transformational leadership, laissez- faire, and bureaucratic leadership.

Carassco-Saul et al. (2015) viewed charismatic leadership as a leadership style in which leaders inspire, attract, and inspire followers by their personal qualities. A good characteristic of charismatic leadership is that it enhances employee satisfaction, thereby stimulating employees to accomplish organizational goals (Carassco-Saul et al., 2015). According to Dwibedi, 2016, charismatic leadership is an identifiable leadership style that may be perceived with less tangibility than other leadership styles. Charismatic leadership is the most successful trait-driven leadership style in which the leader has the vision and personality that inspires followers to achieve the organization's mission (Amegayibor, 2021).

The autocratic leadership style is a classical leadership approach in which the leader retains as much power and decision-making authority as possible (Khanetal, 2015). In this case, the manager does not consult employees when making decisions (khan et al., 2015). Followers are expected to obey orders without any explanations. The motivation environment is created by establishing a structured set of rewards and punishments (khan et al., 2015). The autocratic leadership style is applied where there is little time for group decision-making, or the leader is the most knowledgeable member of the group (Khanetal, 2015). According to Perkins (2020), the autocratic leadership style is a control and command approach in which the leader makes decisions with little or no input from followers. This style can lead to domineering and controlling leadership but could lead to switching decisions when time is of the essence (Perkins, 2020). Also, autocratic leadership is a style that is characterized by individual control overall decisions with little input from team members (Gadirajurrett et al., 2018). In this case, the leader makes decisions based on his idea and judgment without receiving any input from other team members (Gadirajurrett et al., 2018). Transactional leadership is characterized by a reciprocal process between the leader and followers, where compliance with the leader's demands is achieved through an exchange (Carassco-Saul et al., 2015). However, this style does not generate enthusiasm or commitment towards a common goal (Carassco-Saul et al., 2015). Within transactional leadership, there are two approaches: contingent reward, which offers rewards for meeting expectations, and management by exception, which focuses on addressing deviations from established standards (Carassco-Saul et al., 2015). The transactional leadership style assumes that team members agree to obey their leader upon accepting a job offer, and in return, the organization compensates them for their effort and compliance. In this style, the leader has the authority to reprimand team members if their work falls below the established standard (Dwibedi, 2016). Transactional leadership is an exchange process that results in follower compliance with the leader's request but is not likely to generate enthusiasm and commitment to the task objective (Gadirajurrett et al., 2018). The leader ensures that the required tasks are performed by internal factors for the organization to reach its desired goals (Gadirajurrett et al., 2018).

Democratic leadership style is also known as participative leadership style. It encourages employees to be part of decision-making (Khan et al., 2015). In this style, the leader keeps their followers informed about everything that affects their work and thus shares decision-making responsibilities (Khanetal., 2015). This style requires the leader to be a good coach who has no final say but gathers information from staff members before making a decision (Khan et al., 2015). Democratic leadership is a leadership style in which the leader considers and values inputs from team members and peers (Gadirajurrett et al., 2018). This leadership style is also known as participative or shared leadership. In democratic leadership, the leader keeps their followers informed about everything that affects their work and shares the responsibilities for decision-making and problem-solving with the followers (Khan et al., 2015). Democratic leadership usually results in high-quality and high-quantity work in the long run (khan et al., 2015). Furthermore, democratic leadership is a style in which the leader influences the followers strongly and encourages feedback (Allahverdyan & Galstyan, 2016). The democratic leader also guides group members and encourages them to participate in decision-making (kilicoglu, 2018).

Transformational leadership is a leadership style characterized by leaders inspiring and motivating followers through the communication of appealing visions, shared goals, and common values (Carassco-Saul et al., 2015). Leaders in this style also serve as role models, exhibiting desired behaviors for their followers to emulate (Carassco-Saul et al., 2015). The essence of transformational leadership lies in the leader's ability to recognize the need for change, create a vision to guide that change, inspire and motivate others to commit to the vision, and successfully execute the desired transformation (Assen, 2018). Furthermore, transformational leadership places significant emphasis on the development of individuals and groups (Amegayibor, 2021). Extensive research has been conducted on transformational leadership, which offers a comprehensive perspective that complements other leadership models (Amegayibor, 2021).

Laissez-faire leadership is a leadership style that is characterized by non-involvement, showing indifference, and overlooking achievements and problems. It is a leadership style that offers very little direction and allows group members to make decisions independently (Carassco- Saul et al., 2015). In this leadership style, the leader offers little guidance, leaving decisions to the group (Perkins, 2020). This style could lead to high productivity where the team members are self-motivated, but it can also lead to blame, poorly defined roles, and a lack of progress (Perkins, 2020). The laissez-faire leadership style is also known as the 'hands-off' style (Khan et al., 2015). It is a style in which the leader provides little or no direction and gives employees as much freedom as possible (khan et al., 2015). In the laissez-faire leadership style, the leader gives all authority and power to the followers in order to determine goals, makes decisions, and solves problems (Khan et al., 2015).

Bureaucratic leadership, according to Khan et al. (2015), involves the leader managing established procedures and desiring strict adherence to them. This leadership style is particularly suited to situations where employees are engaged in repetitive tasks. Dwibedi (2016) further explains that bureaucratic leaders strictly follow the rules and ensure that their followers also adhere to procedures accurately. Additionally, Arshad et al. (2021) note that bureaucratic leaders consistently abide by the rule of law and diligently enforce its implementation. The foundation of bureaucratic leadership lies in hierarchical roles, a clear chain of command, and the pursuit of

Leadership Skills

According to Khoshnal and Guraya (2016), leadership entails clearly articulating a roadmap and motivating followers to direct their efforts towards achieving desired goals. Additionally, a leader should possess the capability to extract exceptional accomplishments from ordinary individuals. Inherent leadership skills provide a significant advantage to a leader when fulfilling their responsibilities. Khoshhal and Guraya (2016) also emphasize that key leadership skills involve the creation of a vision and a sense of community to inspire others towards excellence. Furthermore, Thompson et al. (2019) conducted relevant empirical studies to examine the leadership skills necessary for effectively leading subordinates.

Psychological researchers on leadership have emphasized the leadership skills required for enhancing significant improvements in business organizations since the beginning of the 20th century (Thompson et al., 2019). A genuine leader is expected to possess desirable qualities such as competency, intelligence, honesty, inspiration, fair-mindedness, broad-mindedness, courage, etc. (Khoshnal & Guray, 2016). The skills required to be possessed by a leader involve strong judgment, sound communication, negotiation, leading by role modeling, the ability to convince and be convinced, and strong confidence skills (Khoshnal & Guraya, 2016).

The Concept of Transformational Leadership

One of the leadership styles that leaders adopt is transformational leadership. Transformational leadership is a people-oriented leadership style that inspires employees to perform beyond expectations for the sake of the organization (Apridar & Adamy, 2018). Transformational leadership enhances employees' satisfaction by imparting a clear vision, mission, and values to their followers (Paleczek et al., 2018). Leaders who adopt synergy, mutual respect, communication, and delegation to attain individual and collective organizational goals are regarded as transformational leaders (Khan et al., 2020). Transformational leadership is unique from other leadership styles because it motivates followers through inspiration (Qabool &Jalees, 2017).

Research evidence has shown that transformational leadership creates an atmosphere of trust and engagement, enhancing employee satisfaction (Qabool & Jalees, 2017). Also, transformational leadership is related to many performance indicators, including employees' commitment and satisfaction (Boies et al., 2015). Transformational leaders not only influence their followers through the exchange of relationships but also stimulate employees' rewards and punishments (Qabool & Jalees, 2017). Consequently, transformational leaders tend to raise their followers' morality and satisfaction levels (Qabool&Jalees,2017). Transformational leadership is a complex and dynamic process in which leaders influence their followers' values, beliefs, and goals (Korejan & Shahbaz, 2016). These leaders move organizations toward the future, recognize environmental needs, and facilitate appropriate changes (Korejan & Shahbaz, 2016). They also create perspectives of potential opportunities for employees and develop a commitment to change, culture improvement, and the need to design new strategies for the efficient use of resources (korejan & Shahbaz, 2016).

Components of Transformational Leadership

According to Long et al. (2014), transformational leaders establish effective communication channels and actively engage in additional efforts with their colleagues and subordinates. They aim to achieve exceptional performance by utilizing various techniques encompassing any combination of the four components of transformational leadership. The components of transformational leadership have emerged due to confinements in concepts and measurement of transformational leadership to a large extent (Long et al., 2014).

Transformational leadership can be linked to ethical and moral values in stimulating the motivational behaviors of followers (Alirezai et al., 2017; Banks et al., 2016).

Transformational leadership refers to the leadership style in which the leader moves the followers beyond immediate self-interests through charisma, inspiration, intellectual stimulation, or individual consideration (Rose & Mamabolo, 2019). Transformational leaders are charismatic, and they pursue goals with their followers. Therefore, transformational leaders are emulated by their followers. Also, transformational leaders inspire followers to overcome the organization's challenges (Long et al., 2014). Transformational leadership consists of four components: idealized influence, inspirational motivation, intellectual stimulation, and individualized consideration (Long et al., 2014).

Idealized Influence

As noted by Long et al. (2014), transformational leaders demonstrate qualities that enable them to lead through their own actions. They are held in high regard and trusted by their followers, acknowledging and appreciating their followers' exceptional skills, determination, and perseverance. Long et al. (2014) highlight two components of idealized influence: the leader's behavior and the inherent qualities attributed to the leader by their followers. These components are seamlessly integrated into the leader's actions, reassuring the followers that the organization's challenges will be overcome. According to Akparobore and Omosekejimi (2020), the leader's effective and clear communication of vision and goals fosters acceptance and enhances follower satisfaction. Additionally, Ama and Oyetunde (2020) assert that the leader's responsibility is to uphold high ethical and moral values within the organization, instilling a sense of purpose among the followers.

Idealized influence helps the followers appreciate the leader's ethical and moral values, thereby earning deeper respect (Asad & Nawab, 2020). Asad and Nawab argued further that idealized influence establishes a friendly atmosphere that reinforces empowerment and ownership responsibility among the followers. Empowerment refers to the satisfaction level justified by McClelland's theory of needs. It emphasizes that attaining power is an influential peer motivation (Braumandl et al., 2020). Idealized influence refers to leaders who act as role models to their followers because they possess extraordinary capabilities and high doctrines of ethical conduct (Reza, 2019). Transformational leaders behave in ways that make them serve as role models to their followers and are admired, respected, and trusted (Reza, 2019). Idealized influence is a charismatic element of transformational leadership (Gonfa, 2019). Gonfa (2019) states that charisma is the capability to inspire a new vision. Transformational leaders have the potential to demonstrate behaviors that serve as role models to their followers (Gonfa, 2019).

They have a strong and clear set of values followed by appropriate actions and greatly influence their followers to make positive changes and differences because of their commitment to ethical values (Gonfa, 2019).

Inspirational Motivation

According to Long et al. (2014), transformational leaders inspire and motivate their followers by fostering team spirit, enthusiasm, and positive thinking. These leaders also establish communication expectations that align with the followers' goals and shared vision. Urbano et al. (2019) further emphasize that transformational leaders exhibit inspirational motivation by effectively communicating goals and providing a clear vision of how to achieve them. Additionally, subordinates often perceive transformational leaders as creative, open-minded, innovative, committed, energized, team-oriented, accomplished, and empowering (Urbano et al., 2019). Jakubik (2020) also maintains that transformational leaders can enhance employee satisfaction by inspiring subordinates to commit to common goals rather than building individual ones.

Inspirational motivation involves leaders' ability to motivate followers so that they can perform beyond expectations (Reza, 2019). Transformational leaders motivate and inspire their followers by giving meaning and challenging their followers' work (Reza, 2019). This is achieved by ensuring no conflict between individual goals and the organizational goal as a whole (Lambert, 2020). Also, inspirational motivation is one of the building blocks of transformational leadership, and transformational leaders behave in ways that motivate and inspire their followers (Gonfa, 2019). Transformational leaders are inspirational individuals who continuously motivate and inspire their followers to key into new ideas (Gonfa, 2019).

Intellectual Stimulation

Transformational leaders are expected to complement their followers' efforts by questioning assumptions, reframing setbacks, and approaching problems in new ways (Long et al., 2014). There is no criticism of the followers' mistakes, and creativity is thus enhanced. The leader solicits new thoughts and creative problem resolution strategies from followers who possess exceptional problem-solving skills (Long et al., 2014). Followers are not criticized when they differ from leaders' ideas (Long et al., 2014). Also, the job characteristics model of Oldham and Hackman supports the argument that employees' satisfaction is gained through experience derived from task variety and tax significance (George & Akinwale, 2020). Nimran et al. (2020) argued that followers at lower levels of the organization lack the capacity to promote innovative processes.

Robinson and Fiset (2020) also argued that followers at lower levels are often seen as enforcers of standards to protect the organization's identity rather than being regarded as innovators. Former et al. (2020) also asserted that leaders can frame tasks in challenging ways for the followers to create a stimulating environment for them. Transformational leaders stimulate their supporters' efforts to be innovative and creative by questioning expectations, reframing difficulties and imminent new ideas (Reza, 2019). Intellectual stimulation involves the stimulation of the followers by the leader to think through issues and problems for themselves and thus develop their abilities (Riza, 2019). Also, intellectual stimulation refers to the ability of transformational leaders to stimulate their followers' efforts to be creative and innovative by questioning assumptions, reframing problems, and approaching old situations in new ways (Gonfa, 2019). Additionally, intellectual stimulation explains the extent to which leaders stimulate their followers' creativity and innovative ability (Gonfa, 2019).

Individualized Consideration

Transformational leaders demonstrate their commitment to the growth and development of their followers by taking on the role of a coach or mentor (Long et al., 2014). They provide support and guidance to help their colleagues and followers reach their full potential. This leadership style promotes individualized consideration, where leaders actively seek out new opportunities for their followers (Long et al., 2014). By fostering two-way communication and employing a hands-on management approach, transformational leaders encourage effective listening and task delegation to facilitate the growth of their followers (Long et al., 2014). They also ensure that the assigned tasks are properly guided and monitored (Long et al., 2014). In the context of transformational leadership, leaders give special attention to each follower's personal and professional growth and help them achieve desired outcomes by acting as mentors or coaches (Reza, 2019). This approach involves creating a supportive climate that fosters individualized consideration and offers new learning opportunities (Reza, 2019). Additionally, individualized consideration is a characteristic of transformational leadership that reflects the qualities of a compassionate leader (Gonfa, 2019). Transformational leaders acknowledge individuals' unique needs and desires and emphasize addressing those needs (Gonfa, 2019).

Delegating tasks is one-way considerate leader develops their followers (Gonfa, 2019).

Individualized consideration is an approach to developing and supporting employees' growth in the context of organizational goals (Alharbi et al., 2020). According to Alharbi et al. (2020), individualized consideration is crucial in enhancing employee satisfaction by addressing individual needs. This approach creates a stable platform for employee development, thereby promoting their self-actualization needs, as argued by Oswald (2019). In order to align the individual needs of followers with those of the organization, leaders must exercise emotional intelligence, as Ntayi et al. (2019) emphasized. Delegating authority to foster personal growth through challenges and experiences promotes a sense of responsibility and ownership among followers, as stated by Ludvik and Nolan-Aranez (2018). It is important for leaders to consistently reassure followers that their individual needs are taken care of, as highlighted by Odeh et al. (2021). These claims are supported by the job characteristics model of Oldham, Hackman, and Herzberg's two-factor model, as mentioned by Odeh et al. (2021).

Transformational Leadership Process

Transformational leadership involves factors, characteristics, and tasks that enable leaders to face current and future challenges and effectively manage the organizational changes resulting from continuous external changes (Alessa, 2021). Through the strength of their vision and personality, transformational leaders can inspire followers to change expectations, perceptions, and motivations to work towards common goals (Bradley, 2020). The adaptation of a company to change determines its sustainability (Thompson, 2021). Many organizations approach the issue of change by simply ignoring it or adopting a step-by-step approach (Thompson, 2021). Transformational leadership embraces dynamism in both company culture and employee mindset to achieve the company's overall objectives (Thompson, 2021).

Transformational leadership is a leadership style in which leaders encourage, inspire and motivate employees to innovate and create change that will help grow and shape the organization's future success (Imran et al., 2016). The transformational leadership processes include leading by example, motivating employees, developing intellectual capacity, and aligning individual objectives with the company's objective (Thompson, 2021). Leading by example is the first step in becoming a transformational leader and influencing the ideas of the people they supervise. This implies that the leader must possess good qualities worthy of emulation, which inspires the followers in the right direction (Thompson, 2021). The motivation of followers is the second step involved in transformational leadership. There is a need for a leader to understand the factors that motivate their followers. For instance, an employee may be motivated by a huge bonus, while another may be motivated by promotion prospects (Thompson, 2021). The third step involved in transformational leadership is to stimulate the followers intellectually. Transformational leaders encourage employees to find new and more efficient ways of handling problems (Thompson, 2021). However, the last step ensures that transformational leaders align the success and fulfillment of employees with the company's mission (Thompson, 2021). Transformational leaders recognize the organization's and staff's needs and stimulate and provide higher-level needs for employees (Korejan & Shabaz, 2016). Transformational leaders encourage employees to work together in pursuit of higher goals to achieve positive important change in an organization (Korejan & Shahbaz, 2016)

Antecedents of Transformational Leadership

Leadership theories were influenced by various academic thoughts, such as business leadership theories, new philosophies, and social thoughts, which led to the emergence of transformational leadership (Meng, 2021). Transformational leadership is the most influential and respected leadership style in management practice (Meng, 2022). Transformational leadership is one of the oldest psychological and methodological approaches used to understand and interpret leadership (Alessa, 2021). The emergence of transformational leadership dates back to 1978, when Burns addressed the distinction between transactional and transformational leadership. He emphasized that transactional leaders attempt to satisfy the current needs of the followers by focusing attention on exchanges. In contrast, transformational leaders attempt to raise the needs of followers and promote dramatic changes in individuals, groups, and organizations (Alessa, 2021). Transformational leadership can be linked to three antecedents: the leader's qualities, the organizational features, and the followers' characteristics (Sun et al., 2017). The leader's qualities refer to the self-efficacy, traits, values, and emotional intelligence of the leader Sun et al., 2017). The organizational features encompass the fairness of the organizational management to employees, while the followers' characteristics refer to the followers' initial developmental level (Sun et al., 2017).

Sun et al. (2017) argued that there are three antecedents of transformational leadership: leaders' internal qualities, organizational factors, and leaders' colleagues' characteristics. They argued further that leaders' self-efficacy, values, emotional intelligence, and cognitive capacities were predictors of transformational leadership at the internal level. For the outcomes that were investigated only by a single empirical study, collaborative cultures between the leader and followers and organizational fairness were positively correlated to transformational leadership (Sun et al., 2017). Supportive, positive, collaborative socialization with colleagues is key to developing transformational leadership. Followers' qualities, such as emotional intelligence and development levels, also influenced the manifestation of transformational leadership (Sun et al., 2017). As the most-studied leadership style in both the Western world and the Chinese context, transformational leadership can potentially suit diverse national and cultural contexts (Jingping et al., 2017). Given that the growing evidence shows the positive effects of transformational leadership on various outcomes, transformational leadership is related to a leader's qualities, organizational fairness, and colleagues' characteristics (Jingping et al., 2017). Some antecedents were common to national and cultural contexts, while others seemed to be national context specific (Jingping et al., 2017).

Relationship between transformational leadership and Employees' Satisfaction

Transformational leadership is a process by which the leaders and followers work with each other to achieve higher satisfaction (El-Toufaili, 2017). Employee satisfaction refers to the overall feelings of employees concerning their jobs (Vandavasi et al., 2020). Employees develop attitudes toward their jobs by considering their feelings, behaviors, and beliefs (Stromberg & Vidman, 2020). Transformational leadership is highly significant because it aligns personal and organizational outcomes (El-Toufaili, 2017). El-Toufaili (2017) argued that transformational leadership has a significant positive relationship with employee satisfaction. He argued further that if leaders and followers can work together based on trust, it will enhance a greater recognition of organizational goals and values, stimulating higher employee satisfaction in the long run. Thus, the extent of employees' satisfaction can be increased by adopting transformational leadership. The success of any organization depends largely on the extent to which it encourages employee satisfaction (Portela et al., 2020).

Satisfied employees demonstrate a greater level of commitment to both their individual jobs and the organization as a whole (Taufer et al., 2020). When employees are satisfied, it positively impacts their efficiency levels, ultimately contributing to the organization's overall success (Neve et al., 2019). According to Rakowska and De Juana-Espinosa (2018), transformational leaders build trust, establish relationships, and provide support to their followers, leading to enhanced satisfaction among them. Transformational leaders achieve this by imparting their followers a clear vision, mission, and values (Pateczek et al., 2018).

Transformational leaders further increase satisfaction levels by inspiring and motivating their followers to perform exceptionally (Vasconcelos, 2018). Effective and transparent communication of the organization's vision and goals also significantly fosters higher satisfaction and acceptance among followers (Akparobore & Omosekejimi, 2020).

Importance of Job Satisfaction

Job satisfaction has been a subject of great interest for researchers and practitioners (Loannou et al., 2015). It refers to an employee's attitude and perception towards their job and its associated activities (Kasemsap, 2017). Employees' level of job satisfaction plays a crucial role in shaping their behaviors towards the organization (Oparinde et al., 2019). Retaining loyal employees is highly dependent on job satisfaction, making it a significant factor for organizations (Kasemsap, 2017). Consequently, organizations are encouraged to adopt systematic management and leadership strategies to enhance employee satisfaction (Kasemsap, 2017). This is because satisfied employees tend to exhibit higher levels of job performance (Kasemsap, 2017). Therefore, improving employee satisfaction stands as one of the most important tasks for organizational management (Ozpehlivan & Acan, 2015). Satisfied employees are also known to transmit positive emotions to customers, thereby contributing to improved organizational profits (Yee et al., 2015).

Managers play a key role in balancing job demands and resources within the job environment (Seljemo et al., 2020). Transformational leadership styles positively influence Employees' satisfaction, engagement, and psychosocial work environment, which reduces adversity in the workplace (Seljemo et al., 2020). Employee satisfaction is one of the utmost goals of all human resource personnel (Bathena,2018). A satisfied employee is not just a retained employee but an ambassador for promoting a company's brand (Bathena, 2018). Employees who are satisfied with their jobs tend to be more loyal to the company and its objectives and go the extra mile to achieve a wide organizational goal (Bathena, 2018). Job satisfaction refers to the inner fulfillment and pride achieved when performing a particular job (Kasemsap, 2017). The work and work environment features can predict the extent of job satisfaction in modern organizations (Brawley & Pury, 2016). Job satisfaction also assists employees in reducing employee turnover and improving their well-being and quality of care (Seljemo et al.,2020). High job satisfaction improves organizational productivity and reduces job stress in modern organizations (Kasemsap, 2017). Job satisfaction also enhances the positive ambiance at the workplace and is essential for ensuring higher revenue for the organization (Kasemsap, 2017).

Measurement of Job Satisfaction

There are numerous measures of job satisfaction. These include the overall job satisfaction measure, job description index, global job satisfaction measure, job satisfaction relative to expectations, Minnesota satisfaction questionnaire, the job in general scale, job satisfaction survey, etc. (Kumar, 2017). Overall Job Satisfaction Measure is a measure of job satisfaction, which is a component of the Michigan Organizational Assessment Questionnaire. In this measure, three items are used to describe an employee's response to working in a specific job and organization (Kumar, 2017).

The job Descriptive Index is a measure of job satisfaction and contains 72 items. The 72 items are used to examine five facets of job satisfaction, including work, pay, promotion, supervision, and co-workers. A comprehensive measure of job satisfaction is developed by combining the ratings of satisfaction with the facets (Kumar, 2017).

Global Job Satisfaction Measure is a measure that uses 15 items to assess overall job satisfaction. It also uses two sub-scales to measure the intrinsic and extrinsic aspects of the job. The intrinsic has seven items, while the extrinsic has eight (Kumar, 2017). Job Satisfaction Relative to Expectation is a measure used to determine the degree of association between the perceived quality of a job and employees' expectations. This measure is most suitable for determining how job stresses, role conflicts, and role ambiguities can hinder an employee from meeting the requirements of the job (Kumar, 2017).

Minnesota Satisfaction Questionnaire is a measure of job satisfaction. It contains 100 questions based on 20 sub-scales that benchmark employees' satisfaction capacity utilization, achievement, activity enhancement, authority, company policies, creativity, recognition, responsibility, moral values, social status, security, human relations, social service, and working conditions (Kumar, 2017). This can also be sub-divided into intrinsic and extrinsic satisfaction (Kumar, 2017).

Job in General Scale is a measure of job satisfaction that contains 18 items which

which measures satisfaction with five job facets (Kumar, 2017). Job in general scale was designed to assess global satisfaction independent from satisfaction with facets (Kumar, 2017). Job Satisfaction Survey was developed based on nine job facets. The job facets include pay, promotion, supervision, benefits, contingent rewards, operating procedures, co-workers, nature of work, and communication (Kumar, 2017). It is used for the assessment of job satisfaction in human service, non-profit, and public organizations (Kumar, 2017). Job Satisfaction Index is a measure of job satisfaction that contains six items that determine overall job satisfaction. These items include work, supervision, co-workers, pay, promotion, opportunities, and the job in general (Kumar, 2017).

The Effect of Transformational Leadership on Employees' Satisfaction in the United States Banking Sector

The banking sector is the bedrock of the majority of contemporary societies (Sinha & Agarwal, 2022). The sector has undergone intense and striking changes in the last few decades due to globalization, privatization, liberalization, and other major global reforms (Sinha & Agarwal, 2022). The rapid change in technology, market demand and financial policies and trade policies impact the level of satisfaction of bank employees (Soni & Agarwal, 2020). The banking sector is a key component of an economy that performs an intermediation role between the depositor and the users of funds (Magasi, 2021). The banking sector stimulates the global economy more than ever since it stabilizes financial systems, facilitates the free flow of funds, and ensures the efficient allocation of financial resources (Magasi, 2021). The banking sector is expected to maintain sound, healthy and stable business through suitable leadership styles such

Transformational leadership is the current design for many financial institutions, which manifests how leaders in banks could impact psychological and behavioral repercussions of their followers (Abouraia & Othman, 2017). The banking sector is not only required to empower employees in terms of attitudes, skills, knowledge, and experience but also to enhance employees' satisfaction levels to attain superior performance (Magasi, 2021). The United States banking sector is dominated by four large banks: JP Morgan Chase, Bank of America, Wells Fargo, and Citigroup. These four banks are not only leading domestically but are also among the largest banks around the world (Norrestad, 2021). Despite the volatile nature of banking operations, this research investigated the impact of transformational leadership on employee satisfaction in the United States banking sector and the influence of collaboration between the leaders and followers on employees' satisfaction since there is a limited research in this area in the United States.

Transformational Leadership and Employees' Performance

Kalsoom et al. (2018) assert that leadership is a core managerial quality that effectively impacts organizational performance and success. Among various leadership styles, transformational leadership is found to be highly related to employees' performance (Kalsoom et al., 2018). Transformational leaders create a strong relationship with their followers in order to motivate, empower and inspire them to attain higher levels of performance (Kalsoom et al., 2018). Transformational leaders are expected to pay attention to each follower with different needs sunder different professional backgrounds and provide opportunities for employees to develop sustainably (Jang et al., 2017). Performance refers to the stage of achievement attained by an individual while undertaking a job in an organization (Eliyana et al., 2015) Employee performance is the capacity of an individual to accomplish a set goal efficiently (Kalsoom et al., 2018). Performance could also be interpreted to mean the productivity level of an employee in comparison with their peers (Buil et al., 2019). The level of performance attained by employees refers to the right quality of work, which can lead to employee satisfaction (Hasib et al., 2020). Employees in the workplace require different levels of support to accomplish a set target. Thus, a transformational leader is expected to realize this and provide coaching and mentoring support to help the followers attain their goals (Mittal & Dhar, 2015). Buil et al. (2019) argued that transformational leadership provides organizational performance-related benefits. Transformational leaders encourage their followers to address personal interests and align them with organizational interests, set high-performance standards, and assist followers to be more creative and innovative, thereby enhancing employees' satisfaction (Buil et al., 2019). Transformational leaders usually motivate followers to achieve performance levels that exceed expectations by changing the values, beliefs, and attitudes of the followers (Hasib et al., 2020).

The Effect of Collaboration between Leaders and Followers on Employees' Satisfaction

A high-quality relationship between the leader and followers is expected to generate positive outcomes (Salas-Vallina, 2020). In the current highly competitive environment, many scholars and practitioners have become increasingly interested in managing leader-follower collaborations (Thompson & Glaso, 2018). A good follower is expected to trust and rely on the leader, show enthusiasm, reveal dependence, and to a certain extent, try to follow their leader's ideas and behave in a civil way toward other employees at work (Alvesson et al., 2016). A positive connection between the leader and the followers is expected to improve positive engagement attitudes, job satisfaction, and effective organizational commitment (Salas- Vallina, 2020). Furthermore, collaboration between the leader and the followers helps reduce friction between them, thereby increasing their quality of life and positive perceptions at work (Salas- Vallina, 2020).

It is important to build a collaborative culture that will strengthen an organization to improve employee satisfaction (Martin, 2021). The understanding of complex situations can be fostered through collaborative teamwork (Martin, 2021). Collaboration helps to develop team interactions that facilitate the learning rate of team members through continuous explanations of viewpoints (Martin, 2021). Over the last few years, leader-follower collaboration has been the main approach for exploring organizational relationships (Martin, 2021). Positive collaboration between leaders and followers benefits individuals and organizations, including employee satisfaction (Salas-Vallina, 2020). Research shows that collaboration between leaders and followers is predisposed to stimulate employee satisfaction (Salas-Vallina, 2020). Job satisfaction refers to objectively evaluating employees' feelings about working conditions such as salary, career development, promotion, etc. (Salas-Vallina, 2020). The collaboration between leaders and followers fosters a sense of belongingness for the followers, thereby enhancing employees' satisfaction (Salas-Vallina, 2020). Positive collaboration between the leader and followers is expected to improve positive attitudes of engagement and employee satisfaction (Salas-Vallina, 2020). Collaboration within an organization is an interpersonal approach among individuals based on their social and organizational structures in order to achieve common goals (Kilicoglu, 2018). This will make the leaders to be well-equipped about the key outcomes of their decisions (Kilicoglu, 2018).

Conditions under which Transformational Leadership becomes Successful in relation to Employees' Satisfaction

For transformational leadership to succeed, the leader must be visionary and instill a culture that encourages the followers to perform their roles in the company's best interest (Gonfa, 2019). Because transformational leadership covers a wide range of aspects within leadership, there are no specific steps for a leader to follow (Wysocki et al., 2022). Becoming a transformational leader is a procedural process, which implies that a conscious effort must be made to adopt a transformational leadership style (Wysocki et al., 2022).

Understanding the basics of transformational leadership can help a leader successfully apply this style (Wysocki et al., 2022). Transformational leadership is a style of leadership in which the leader identifies the needed change, creates a vision to guide the change, and executes the change (Gonfa, 2019). Transformational leadership is about change, and the change focuses on altering organizational mission, vision, values, and performance to achieve maximum efficiency and quality in product and service delivery (Gonfa, 2019). Transformational leadership is a leadership style in which the leader encourages, inspires, and motivates followers to create a desirable change for the organization (White, 2018). This could be accomplished by setting a realistic example at the executive level by developing good corporate culture, employee ownership, and interdependence in the workplace (White, 2018).

A transformational leader must encourage followers to act in the best interest of the company and should be a strong role model with high values (Wysocki et al., 2022). A transformational leader creates a vision, acts as an agent of change within the organization by setting good examples of how to initiate and implement change and helps the organization to achieve the desired goals by helping followers to contribute to the organization (Wysockietal., 2022). It is pertinent to mention that transformational leadership is an iterative process covering many aspects. The first condition that must be met to enhance the success of transformational leadership is to understand the basics of transformational leadership as well as its four components (White, 2018). According to White (2018), in order for transformational leadership to be effective, it is crucial to provide employees with training that empowers them to take charge of decision-making within their assigned roles. By offering greater opportunities for creativity and forward-thinking, employee satisfaction can be enhanced. Additionally, White (2018) suggests that individuals on a leadership trajectory can be equipped to become transformational leaders through a combination of training and mentoring.

Empirical Review

Review of Previous Literature on Transformational Leadership

There is no prior study on the effect of transformational leadership on employee satisfaction in the United States banking sector. This research represents the first attempt to explore this particular area. However, this section reviews previous literature regarding transformational leadership's impact on employee satisfaction across different countries. By doing so, it aims to gain a better understanding of how transformational leadership affects the satisfaction of employees in the banking sector. Ali et al. (2016) conducted a study to examine the influence of transformational leadership on job satisfaction and organizational commitment. They utilized a structured questionnaire administered to 126 employees working in the banking sector of Peshawar. The findings indicated a significant positive impact of transformational leadership on both job satisfaction and organizational commitment.

Similarly, Baffour-Awuah and Agyei (2020) investigated the effects of transformational and transactional leadership styles on job satisfaction at Cape Coast Technical University. Their findings provided evidence that both transformational and transactional leadership styles enhance job satisfaction among faculty members of the institution. Another study by Duyan and Yidiz (2020) explored the impact of transformational leadership on job satisfaction within the faculties of sports sciences in Turkey. The results revealed a significant and positive relationship between transformational leadership and job satisfaction.

Abelha et al. (2018) conducted a study to investigate the impact of transformational leadership on job satisfaction. The results of their research revealed a noteworthy and positive correlation between transformational leadership and employee satisfaction. Similarly, Nzelibe and Yasar (2015) conducted a study to assess the effects of transformational management on employees' satisfaction, workgroup supportiveness, commitment, and performance at both the individual and organizational levels. The findings of their study indicated a significant and positive relationship between transformational leadership and employee satisfaction in Nigeria. Another study by Tuan and Rajagopal (2019) examined the influence of the transformational leadership style on employee satisfaction in small and medium-sized enterprises in Ho Chi Minh City, Vietnam. The outcome of their research suggested that transformational leadership has a positive impact on employee satisfaction in Vietnam.

Safrizal and Usman (2020) examined the effect of transformational leadership on employees' satisfaction in Ikan Bakar Cianjur restaurant in Surabaya. The research evidence revealed that transformational leadership exerts a significant positive influence on employee satisfaction. Khan et al. (2018) investigated the impact of transformational leadership on employees' job satisfaction and well-being through team efficacy in Punjab Model Bazaar Company. The research evidence revealed that transformational leadership positively impacts employees' job satisfaction. Hasib et al. (2020) studied the effect of transformational leadership on employee performance mediated by the leader member exchange in Indonesia. The research evidence revealed that transformational leadership enhances employee satisfaction and performance. Malik et al. (2017) investigated the influence of transformational leadership components on Pakistan's job satisfaction and organizational commitment. The evidence of the findings revealed that transformational leadership components significantly influence job satisfaction and organizational commitment of employees.

Chen et al. (2021) investigated transformational leadership and employee job satisfaction in China. The findings revealed that transformational leadership is positively related to employees' satisfaction via the mediation role of the perceived employee relation climate. Rafia and Sunaryo (2020) examined the effect of transformational leadership on employee performance mediated by job satisfaction. The empirical findings indicated that transformational leadership does not have a direct significant effect on employee performance but has a direct significant effect on job satisfaction. Arumugan et al. (2019) investigated the effect of transactional and transformational leadership styles on employee satisfaction in 377 conglomerate companies. The research evidence suggests that transformational and transactional leadership positively affects employee job satisfaction.

Folmae (2020) investigated transformational leadership and employee satisfaction in a United States fast-food restaurant. The result indicated that transformational leadership positively impacts employees' satisfaction. Thomas (2018) also examined transformational leadership and job satisfaction among Federal Government employees in the United States. The study's findings indicated that transformational leadership has a significant positive impact among the Federal Government employees in the United States. Sun et al. (2017) reviewed the antecedents of transformational leadership in the United States and China. The research evidence suggests that transformational leadership is related to three antecedents, including the leader's qualities, organizational features, and the leader's colleagues' characteristics.

Summary

This review provides robust evidence on the effect of transformational leadership on employees' satisfaction in the United State banking sector. It also explains the different types of leadership styles such as charismatic leadership, autocratic leadership, democratic leadership, transactional leadership, transformational leadership, laissez-faire leadership, and bureaucratic leadership. Among the leadership styles, transformational leadership is preferred because it is a people-oriented leadership style that inspires employees to perform beyond expectations. The research evidence revealed that transformational leadership is connected to three sets of antecedents, namely, the leader's qualities, the organizational features and the followers. The review of relevant literature shows that employees' satisfaction can be enhanced through the adoption of transformational leadership. The success of any organization depends on the extent to which employees' satisfaction is encouraged.

Job satisfaction plays a vital role as it contributes to the retention of loyal employees who can deliver higher levels of job performance. Furthermore, it is crucial for fostering strong collaboration between leaders and followers, promoting effective team interactions, and serving as a solid foundation for employee satisfaction. In the United States banking sector, four major banks, namely JP Morgan Chase, Bank of America, Wells Fargo, and Citigroup, dominate the industry. To ensure the sector's continued success and stability, transformational leadership is expected to be implemented. This involves empowering employees by developing their attitudes, skills, knowledge, and experience, while prioritizing enhancing employee satisfaction to drive performance to new heights.

Chapter 3: Methodology

Introduction

This qualitative descriptive research study investigated the effect of transformational leadership on employee satisfaction in the United States banking sector and the influence of collaborations between the leaders and followers on employees' satisfaction. Studies have revealed that transformational leadership positively affects employee satisfaction in the United States (Folmae, 2020; Thomas, 2018; Sun et al., 2017). Presently, there is a limited research that studies the effect of transformational leadership in the United States banking sector. Thus, this study aimed to fill the literature gap by providing further evidence on the effect of transformational leadership on employee satisfaction in the United States banking sector. The research demonstrated how banks in the United States could enhance employee satisfaction through the adoption transformational leadership, even in the face of challenging economic conditions.

Transformational leadership is a significant element that enhances organizational success through the stimulation of greater involvement in the work of subordinates (El-Toufaili, 2017). In this chapter, the research problem and research questions were identified. The chapter also explained the research methodology, research design, population and sample, instrumentation, research procedures, data analysis, protection of human rights, delimitations and limitations, assumptions, risks and biases, the study's significance, and a summary of the chapter.

Research Methodology

The term "methodology" refers to the systematic and theoretical analysis of the methods applied to a field of study (Igwenagu, 2016). In the context of research, research methodology refers to a set of systematic techniques that guide research and how it is conducted (Igwenagu, 2016). Ultimately, research methodology acts as the pathway through which researchers conduct their studies (Sileyew, 2019). Every research involves an explicit and systematic approach to investigate a given phenomenon (Mohajan, 2018).

Research methodology shows the path through which the research problem and objective are formulated and helps to present data obtained during the study (Sileyew, 2019). However, there are two types of research methodologies: quantitative and qualitative. Quantitative research involves the quantification and analysis of variables in order to obtain results (Apute, 2017). It is the utilization and analysis of numerical data to proffer solutions to research questions based on statistical techniques (Apute, 2017). In quantitative research, data is obtained in order to provide information that could be subjected to statistical treatment, which provides a basis for accepting or rejecting alternative knowledge claims (Apute, 2017).

On the other hand, a qualitative research methodology is an inquiry process that provides an understanding of distinct methodological traditions of inquiry that investigates a specific problem (Isaac, 2014). It refers to a methodology that provides a complex picture, analyzes words, provides comprehensive and detailed views of participants, and executes research in a natural setting (Isaac, 2014). Qualitative research methodology is highly significant, where the researcher targets complex issues influencing human behavior. The goal of qualitative research is to provide a good explanation of the understanding of social phenomena based on the analysis of the views and experiences of all participants (Isaac, 2014). Qualitative research methodology is a form of social action that emphasizes the use of experience to investigate a specific problem (Gopaldas, 2016). It involves using interviews, classroom observations, immersions, and open- ended questionnaires to analyze the data content of visual and textual materials (Mohajan, 2018). Qualitative research is an inductive methodology where the researcher explores meanings and insights in a given situation (Levitt et al., 2017). It is explanatory and explores how a specific phenomenon operates in a given context (Mohajan, 2018). Qualitative research methodology is observing and interpreting people's perceptions in a natural setting (Gentles et al., 2015). This study uses qualitative research because it captures the totality of human experience in providing answers to the research question.

Research Design

One of the most significant tasks in research is selecting an appropriate research design to answer research questions (Doyle et al., 2021). It is essential for researchers to be able to justify their choice of research design in a study (Doyle et al., 2021). Research design encompasses the process of collecting, analyzing, interpreting, and reporting data in research (Igwenagu, 2016). Its purpose is to establish a suitable framework for a study (Sileyew, 2019). In simpler terms, research design serves as the overall plan that connects the conceptual research problems with the relevant empirical research investigation. The research design involves using evidence-based procedures and guidelines that equip researchers with the necessary tools and framework to undertake a study (Majid, 2018). There are various types of research designs, namely experimental research design, case study research design, and descriptive qualitative research design.

Experimental research design is concerned with constructing research that is high in casual validity (Mitchell, 2015). Casual validity examines the accuracy of statements regarding cause-and-effect relationships (Mitchell, 2015). This method is more appropriate for quantitative research but not suitable for qualitative studies because it involves the use of numeric and statistical data to provide answers to research questions (Mitchell, 2015). A case study research design is a research technique that focuses on an in-depth investigation of an individual, group, or phenomenon. A case study research design is more of a research strategy, while a descriptive qualitative research design is not viewed as a strategy but as part of the research (Mitchell, 2015).

Researchers who wish to undertake qualitative research could adopt a wide range of qualitative approaches, as discussed above. However, descriptive qualitative research is most suitable for a study exploring participants' experiences (Doyleetal.,2021).A descriptive qualitative research design is deemed to be most appropriate for analyzing the nature of a problem, the experiences of the participants, and the presentation of findings in a logical manner (Bradshaw etal.,2017).Descriptive qualitative research design is also applicable in studies involving the use of mixed methods where qualitative data can be used to explain quantitative findings (Doyleetal., 2021). It can also be used to develop questionnaires in exploratory studies and validate convergent studies (Doyle et al., 2021). For this study, descriptive qualitative research was used.

This study's use of descriptive qualitative research design made the findings more meaningful (Doyle et al., 2021). From a philosophical point of view, descriptive qualitative research design is best suited for analyzing critical theories that employ naturalistic and interpretative methods (Lincoln et al., 2017). In descriptive qualitative research design, the researcher is concerned with understanding individual human experience in its unique context. (Lincoln et al., 2017). Descriptive qualitative research inquiry requires dynamic research processes that strictly concentrate on the phenomenon of investigation (Doyle et al., 2021). It involves the application of pragmatism to research, which has to do with the application of the best methods to answer the research question (Doyle et al., 2021).

Descriptive qualitative research design recognizes and incorporates uncertainty about the phenomenon of investigation and the research methods used to study the phenomenon (Long et al., 2018). For researchers, it allows the use of one or more types of inquiry, which is essential in acknowledging and examining experiences in relation to a phenomenon being studied (Long et al., 2018). More specifically, the rationale for selecting the methods used by the researcher to investigate a given phenomenon emerges from the deceptive qualitative research design because the data obtained for the study continue to remain close to the phenomenon throughout the study (Doyle et al., 2021).

Population and Sample

A population is a well-defined collection of individuals or objects with similar characteristics (Majid, 2018). It is impossible to collect data from the entire population when undertaking research (Stratton, 2021). This may be because the members of the population cannot be individually identified, or the population is too large to give room for census-based study (Stratton, 2021). A population usually contains many individuals to study conveniently, and as such, an investigation is subjected to one or more samples drawn from the population

(BMJ, 2022). A well-chosen sample usually contains most of the characteristics of a particular population (BMJ, 2022). It is important to have a good relationship between the population and the sample so that inferences can be made about the population from the sample (BMJ, 2022). The first key feature of a sample is that it gives every member of the population a chance to be selected (BMJ, 2022).

One of the fundamental objectives of a research is to obtain a statistically representative sample from the population of interest in such a way that the inferences and findings of the study cannot be attributed to random variations in the population of interest (Majid, 2018). In research, there are different strategies that the researcher can adopt to obtain a representative sample from the population of interest, which is the target population (Majid, 2018). These strategies are known as sampling techniques, and the sampling techniques employed in a study depend on the characteristics of the population of interest, the significance level, and the research questions (Majid, 2018). The target population of this study is composed of all employees who work in the United States banking sector.

The core objective of research is to draw valid conclusions and generalize research objectives from a smaller sample to a larger population (Elfil & Negida, 2017). Statistical methods are employed to achieve this purpose of inference (Elfil & Negida, 2017). A sample refers to a subset of the population that is selected in an unbiased manner to serve as a representative of the entire population (Elfil & Negida, 2017). Utilizing samples in studies is often more cost-effective and practical than studying the entire population (Elfil & Negida, 2017). Determining an appropriate sample size is a practical consideration that needs to be addressed during a study's planning and design stage (Das et al., 2016). The sample size represents a proportion of the population chosen for the study's purpose (Majid, 2018). Due to the impracticality of examining the entire population, researchers draw a sample from the population to conduct their study (Andrade, 2020). It is crucial for the sample to be a reliable representation of the study population (Andrade, 2020).

The sample size is a key component of any qualitative or empirical study on the basis of which inferences will be -deduced for the study. Sample adequacy in qualitative research relates to the suitability of the sample composition and size (Vasileiou et al., 2018). It is an important consideration in the evaluation of the quality of a qualitative study of this nature. Samples in qualitative studies tend to be small in order to support the depth of case-oriented analysis that is key to this mode of research (Vasileiouetal., 2018). The sample size of 25 respondents drawn based on purposive sampling was utilized for the purpose of this study. Sample size sufficiency in qualitative research relates to the appropriateness of the sample composition and size (Vasileiou et al., 2018). It is a key consideration in evaluating the trustworthiness of qualitative research (Vasileiou et al., 2018). Samples in qualitative research are usually small to support the depth of the case-oriented analysis that is significant to this mode of inquiry (Vasileiouetal., 2018). Saturation is the most common method researchers used to justify the sufficiency of sample size (Saunders et al., 2018). Also, saturation has attained global acceptability as a methodological principle in qualitative studies (Saunders et al., 2018). It is commonly used to indicate no need for further data collection and analysis (Saundersetal., 2018). It is a criterion adopted in qualitative research for discontinuing data collection (Saunders et al., 2018).

Saturation is a point in the research process whereby sufficient data has been obtained to draw necessary conclusions, and further data collection will not yield any value-added insights (Faulkner &Trotter, 2017). Saturation implies that a researcher can be reasonably assured that further at a collection will produce similar results and serve to confirm emerging themes and conclusions (Faulkner & Trotter, 2017).Purposive sampling is a technique in which the researcher makes use of his or her judgment in selecting members of the target population that will participate in the study (Benoot et al., 2016).

The logic and power of purposeful sampling lie in its effectiveness in selecting information-rich cases for an in-depth study (Benoot et al., 2016). Information-rich cases are information from which the researcher can learn a lot of issues that are highly significant to the purpose of the study (Benoot et al., 2016). In the study, a total of 25 participants were selected for further examination. Out of this sample size, 15 were subjected to personal interviews, while the remaining 10 were engaged in focus group discussions. Each of the 15 participants underwent a one-hour interview conducted via Zoom.

On the other hand, the 10 participants for the focus group discussions were divided into two groups, each comprising five participants. The focus group discussions were also conducted on Zoom and were recorded for reference. It is worth noting that participation in either the interview or the focus group discussions were voluntary, and no participant was allowed to belong to both groups simultaneously. Therefore, each participant could only be a part of the interview or focus group. The recruitment of the participants was done based on the inclusion criteria. The researcher used inclusion criteria such as a minimum of 10-year working experience in the banking sector, a minimum academic qualification of Associate/Bachelor of Science, and the age bracket of 30 to 45 years to select the sample size of 25 participants. Inclusion criteria are guiding rules that help the researcher identify the study population in a consistent, reliable, uniform, and objective manner (Garg, 2016).

The 10 participants for the focus group discussion were organized into two groups, with each group consisting of five members. All the interview and focus group discussion participants were selected from the United States banking sector. For participant recruitment, an online survey company called Respondents was contracted. The focus group discussion aimed to gain a comprehensive understanding of the impact of transformational leadership on employee satisfaction within the United States banking sector, further validating the previously collected data. Additionally, the focus group discussion aimed to provide additional clarity on specific issues relevant to the study's objectives, as identified by a deliberately chosen group of individuals. The interview and focus group questions were field tested by three experts to discover whether the instruments actually addressed the research topic (Appendix B to D).

The main intent of the focus group discussion was to clarify the data that had already been gathered and to expand upon it. This study used purposive sampling to select 25 participants from the total number of employees working in the United States banking sector. Purposive sampling is a commonly employed technique in qualitative research aimed at identifying and selecting information-rich cases that are relevant to the phenomenon under investigation (Palinkas et al., 2015). This approach involves carefully identifying and selecting individuals or groups with substantial knowledge and experience regarding the phenomenon of interest (Palinkas et al., 2015). Purposive sampling has a long developmental history, and many scholars believe it is simple and straightforward. The reason for purposive sampling is to better match the sample with the aims and objectives of the research, thereby improving the study's rigor and the research's trustworthiness (Campbell et al., 2020).

Data Sources

Instrument refers to a generic term used to represent measurement tools in research (Sathiyaseelan, 2015). The selection of an appropriate research instrument is an important step in the research process (Sathiyaseelan, 2015). The instrument is used to measure the study variables and must be able to capture all variables in terms of its conceptual definition (Sathiyaseelan, 2015). For the purpose of this study, interviews and focus group discussions were used as the research instrument to collect the appropriate data. The researcher obtained some demographic information about the participants, such as the age of the participants, academic qualification, and length of service of the participants in the banking sector, as a basis for determining the inclusion criteria of the participants (Appendix B to C).

The most common method of collecting data in qualitative studies is through interviews (Jamshed, 2014). In qualitative interviews, not only are the practices and standards recorded, but they are also established and reinforced (Jamshed, 2014). The interviews conducted for this study were semi-structured and conducted face-to-face with the participants, alongside focus group discussions (see Appendix B to D). A total of 15 participants were interviewed individually, each lasting 60 minutes, while ten participants were engaged in focus group discussions. The participants were recruited through an online agency called Respondents. To ensure the quality of the interview and focus group questions, an expert panel reviewed them.

This expert review serves as a pretesting method to identify any potential issues with the questions before they are field-tested. In total, three interviews were conducted per day over five days, resulting in a total of 15 interviews. At least two experts were engaged to review the questions before conducting the interview and focus group discussions. After that, field-testing of the interview questions was done through the engagement of three people who represented the population but were not part of the actual sample. These three people were subjected to semi-structured interviews and focus group discussions, and the data obtained from them were transcribed and analyzed to examine if the research questions addressed the research purpose and problem. A semi-structured interview is based on a semi-structured interview guide, which is a schematic presentation of questions by the interviewer (Jamshed, 2014).

The interview guide serves as a tool for data collection from the participants systematically and comprehensively, keeping the interview focused on the subject matter (Jamshed, 2014). The questions in the interview guide comprise the core research questions and other associated questions relevant to the research objectives (Jamshed, 2014). In line with Jamshed (2014), recording of the interviews was done in order to capture the interview data more effectively. The choice of using an interview in this study was motivated by its ability to offer a more comprehensive understanding and elucidate the participants' opinions, behaviors, and experiences (Jamshed, 2014). Conducting interviews allows for a deeper exploration of the participants' perspectives, comprehension, and firsthand encounters related to the research topic, thereby facilitating a thorough collection of data (Jamshed, 2014). Focus group discussions were also used to gain an in-depth understanding of the participants on the effect of transformational leadership on employees' satisfaction in the United States banking sector. The methodology facilitated the acquisition of data from a deliberately chosen group of individuals instead of a statistically representative sample drawn from a larger population (Nyumba et al., 2018).

Research Procedures

Research procedures are various steps through which a research will be conducted. The first research procedure defines the aim of the research, which is the investigation of the effect of transformational leadership on employee satisfaction. The subsequent step involved the selection of the appropriate data collection method. The data collection methods utilized in this study were semi-structured interviews and focus group discussions (Appendix B). Following that, the suitable research design for the study was chosen by the researcher, who employed a descriptive qualitative research design. The subsequent stage entailed the creation of a data management plan for the study, which assisted in organizing and storing the data in a suitable manner for data analysis purposes. The final step in the data collection procedure was to prepare the data for analysis. To accomplish this, data cleaning was conducted.

Data cleaning is the process of detecting and removing errors and inconsistencies in a given set of data. Also, data cleaning consists of error detection and error repair (Chu & Ilyas, 2016). Error repairing was done by applying data transformation scripts or by involving human experts (Chu & Ilyas, 2016). Both error detection and error repair are aimed at improving the quality of data analyzed for the purpose of the study. Data quality is one of the key problems in data management because wrong data usually leads to inaccurate data analysis results (Chu & Ilyas, 2016). To increase the reliability of the study, the researcher sent a notice to the prospective participants to solicit their participation. The researcher met with the prospective participants after the acceptance of the call to participate. The company conducting the online survey (Respondents) obtained the participants' email addresses as part of their responsibility for recruiting the respondents. This enabled the researcher to obtain the informed consent of the participants for the study. A copy of the informed consent form was sent to each participant via email, and the form was signed and forwarded back to the researcher at least two days before the commencement of the interview and focus group discussions (Appendix E)

Thereafter, the prospective participants were made to sign a privacy and confidential agreement. The objective was to guarantee the participants that the information supplied will only be used for the research and will not be divulged to unauthorized third parties. Before the administration of the interview and focus group discussion, the researcher examined the length of service of the participants in the banking sector, the age range of the participants, and their academic background. This enabled the researcher to ensure that the right participants were recruited for this study, and an acceptance notice was sent to them via mail. The researcher then administered the interview questions, and semi-structured interviews were conducted with 15 participants to obtain more information, enabling the researcher to conduct well-detailed research. Furthermore, the remaining 10 participants were subjected to focus group discussions. The discussion was organized via Zoom meeting with the participants, and the discussions were audio and video recorded with the participants' permission. The researcher obtained the participants' email, so the Zoom link was shared before the focus group discussion. Two focus groups were formed, and each group was composed of five members. Discussions were held in the research area, and the outcomes of the discussions were documented for the study.

Data security is essential to maintain a good relationship with the participants and produce quality research output. The researcher endeavored to use the first names of the participants during the administration of the interviews and focus group discussions. This enabled the researcher to easily identify the participants. The names were struck during the transcription of responses obtained from the participants. The researcher also used member checking to enhance the credibility of results by returning the preliminary data to the participants to check for accuracy and resonance with their experience (Linda et al., 2016). Member checking helped in enhancing the credibility of results. The information supplied by the participants was audio taped and transcribed. The conversion of data into written reports is one of the techniques used for managing qualitative data. Qualitative research is usually criticized on the ground that it is biased. However, if the qualitative research is well conducted, it could produce an unbiased, in-depth, reliable, rigorous, and credible result (Anderson, 2020).

Furthermore, it is important in a qualitative study to examine the extent to which claims are supported by convincing evidence. Triangulation involves using two or more methods to study the same phenomenon. In other words, triangulation refers to the use of multiple sources of data in qualitative research to develop a comprehensive analysis of the phenomena (Bhandari, 2022). It is a research strategy that helps the researcher to enhance the viability and credibility of the research findings (Bhandari, 2022). In this study, methodological triangulation was used.
Methodological triangulation involves the use of different methods to approach the research questions. The methodological triangulation was very helpful because it helped to avoid flaws and biases that came with reliance on a single research technique (Bhandari, 2022).

Contradictory evidence, also known as deviant cases, was examined and recognized in the analysis to ensure that the researcher's bias did not interfere with the perception of the data. The continuous comparison also enabled the researcher to identify emerging themes within the study (Anderson, 2010). Bracketing is a method used in qualitative research to reduce the potentially deleterious effects of preconceptions that may jeopardize the research process (Weatherford & Maitra, 2019). Bracketing is a key part of qualitative research used by researchers to mitigate preconceptions related to the research and thereby to increase the study's rigor (Weatherford & Maitra, 2019). Bracketing is a significant component of qualitative research, especially phenomenology and other approaches that require interviews, observations, and focus group discussions (Spirko, 2019). This study involved the use of the mind-mapping method of bracketing. Mind-mapping is a technique of methodological reduction that helps to develop non- judgmental research whose objectivity about the participants will not impede the perception of the phenomenon at the heart of the study (Spirko, 2019). The researcher utilized mind-mapping approaches such as note-taking and brainstorming to remove previous assumptions that could negatively impact the research outcomes.

To analyze the data obtained through interviews and focus group discussions, the transcripts are coded. The coding process involves linking the raw data to theoretical terms, as Bisetto et al. (2020) described. The codes are then organized, summarized, and categorized. This coding and analysis process generates a descriptive theory of the behavioral pattern being studied (Bisetto et al., 2020). Saldana's (2016) method of coding and theming was employed to describe the contents of the interviews and focus group discussion. This method involves identifying, examining, and analyzing the reporting themes within the collected data. Its utilization aims to minimize errors in theming and coding to the greatest extent possible. The coding process is performed using qualitative data management software MaxQDA version 12. The participants were required to be briefed on the research outcome at the end of the study. They were provided with straightforward, concise, and informative explanations regarding the rationale behind the study's design and the methods that were employed.

Project Data Analysis

For the purpose of this study, the researcher employed the use of Saldana's coding and theming method. A theme is defined as an outcome of coding, categorization, and analytic reflection, not something that is, in itself, coded (Saldana, 2016). Saldana's method of coding and theming was used to describe the features of the contents of the interviews and focus group discussion through the identification, examination, and analysis of the reporting themes within the collected data. The research leveraged the themes surrounding the two aforementioned questions by starting with data collection and ending with answering and interpreting the research question. The interview responses were also made using the Saldana coding and theming method. This method was used to identify the study's themes, patterns, and values. These themes and patterns were highly useful in analyzing the participants' feedback. Interviews were transcribed and coded using MaxQDA version 12.

Member checking is a technique used to establish the degree of trustworthiness and credibility in qualitative research (Linda et al., 2016). The trustworthiness of results is the bedrock on which high-quality research lies. Member checking allows participants to review preliminary findings to verify it accurately represent their views, increasing the trustworthiness of outcomes (Carlson, 2010). Member checking is also known as participant validation, a tool for enhancing the credibility of the results (Linda et al., 2016). The interviews were transcribed and sent to the participants for their review via email. This allowed the participants to check their responses and add to the comments should they choose. Carlson (2010) argues that member checking can help increase the member's willingness to participate in a study. In a scenario where the researcher did not receive certain responses, a reminder notice was sent to those participants as a follow-up to ensure that the necessary feedback was obtained. According to Marshall and Rossman (2014), data that provide an alternate perception is a discrepant case. It is easy for a researcher to accept or embrace an initial idea and fail to explore counterevidence. In order to counteract the tendency to rely solely on initial impressions, it is important to maintain balance in the research process. The presence of discrepancies in cases can have an impact on the validity of the study. Therefore, the researcher ensured to identify and appropriately address any divergent cases that arise. Additionally, the theme development phase commenced after the conclusion of the interview and focus group discussion. To facilitate this process, the researcher followed the four-phase theme development process outlined by Vaismoradi et al. (2016). The first phase, initialization, involves transcribing each participant's account entirety while noting any themes or patterns that emerge from the participants' statements and the researcher's reflective notes (Vaismoradi et al., 2016).

The next process is the construction of themes through the definition, classification, comparison, labeling, and translation of the collected data (Vaismoradi et al., 2016). The third stage is analyzing, grouping, and conceptualizing codes that relate to the phenomenon of interest. The last stage refers to the finalization of the development stage (Vaismoradi et al., 2016). This involves the development of narratives that provide a robust view of the phenomenon. The narratives linked themes and subthemes and addressed gaps between the research question and the obtained data (Vaismoradi et al., 2016).

Protection of Human Rights

The researcher ensured that the human rights of the participants were not infringed upon in any way. The confidentiality of the information provided by the respondents in the interviews and focus group discussions was given utmost importance by the researcher. Unauthorized third parties were not granted access to the information solely intended for academic purposes.

Additionally, all citations used in this study were appropriately referenced. The researcher adhered to the highest moral and ethical standards to safeguard the human rights of the participants. Collaborative Institutional Training Initiatives (2015) recommended the cruciality of maintaining participant privacy in any research involving human subjects. Consequently, the researcher took precautionary measures to protect the human rights of the participants.

The protection of all participants was ensured based on IRB established guidelines. The researcher provided an informed consent form to all participants at the beginning of the data collection process, ensuring that they were aware of the research's purpose. Additionally, a statement emphasizing confidentiality and ethical requirements, in accordance with IRB guidelines (Appendix G), was provided to each participant. The selection of participants was conducted with fairness and equity, ensuring that no individual or group of individuals was unfairly included or excluded from the study. The Belmont Report identifies the basic ethical principles that should be complied with in conducting research that involves human subjects

(Czubaruk, 2019). It also sets the guidelines to ensure these basic principles are followed throughout the research process. (Czubaruk, 2019). The Belmont Report serves as a key reference in evaluating the ethical sensitivity of studies involving human participants (Anabo et al., 2019). According to Anabo et al. (2019), the Belmont Report suggests the following recommendations: seeking informed consent, evaluating benefits and risks, and ensuring fair and equitable selection, representation, and burden of participation. The report highlights that failure to adhere to these principles can result in harm, coercion, and undue involvement of vulnerable and burdened subjects.

Furthermore, participants were subjected to interviews respectively and sensitively to eliminate the exposure of the participants to physical or emotional harm. The researcher protected the identity of the participants by using pseudonyms, and participants had the option of ending their voluntary participation at any point in time without any infringement of their rights. Additionally, all the relevant information was submitted to the IRB by the researcher. The IRB requires all researchers to assess the potential risk that could negatively impact the participants in a study, such as physical, social, psychological, legal, economic, etc. (Merriam & Tisdell, 2016). The researcher secured the prior consent of the participants to ensure that the written proposal was accepted. There was also protection of the participant's identity in accordance with the signed consent form obtained before the commencement of the study. Finally, it was important to emphasize that all recorded data would be kept for a period of three years and then destroyed thereafter.

Delimitations and Limitations

Limitations are weaknesses that militate against the study, which are outside the researcher's control and are closely associated with the chosen research design (Theofanidis & Fountouki, 2019). Delimitations are the limitations consciously set by the researcher.

Delimitations emphasize the definitions that the researcher decides to set as the boundaries or limits of their work so that the aims and objectives of the study do not become difficult to achieve (Theofanidis and Fountouki, 2019). Also, delimitation aids the researcher to be more focused on the study with a view to reducing the tendency to work outside research boundaries. The selection of the participants from the United States banking sector further classifies this study's delimitation.

Good research requires a lot of work, but constraints may likely hinder the researcher from carrying out successful research work. In carrying out this work, there had to be adequate time available, but the researcher was constrained by time. Research work of this nature requires a lot of funds. This research work was also characterized by insufficient funds to obtain the required data. The basic raw facts that formed the bedrock of the research were often not readily available. The data was obtained from a primary source through the use of a questionnaire. The researcher played a key role in the data collection process; consequently, the researcher could have made unrealistic assumptions. Reflexivity may shift part of the focus of the study onto the researcher. Reflexivity is the examination of the researcher's judgment, practice, and belief in the process of collecting data (Delve, 2022). It is important to emphasize that the researcher is a dynamic part of the qualitative study and could actively influence the outcome of the study (Delve, 2022). The researcher identified personal beliefs that could have negatively impacted the study's outcome and questioned her assumptions.

Furthermore, there is a possibility that many potential experiences are eliminated by deliberating and choosing the participants that will partake in a study through purposive sampling (Emerson, 2015). This poses a limitation to the study because some new information or data may be missed, which could not be provided by the selected sample of participants. Another limitation of the study emanates from the use of semi-structured interview questions. This type of question can limit the direction of narratives from the participants, which could potentially result in a loss of valuable experience that the participants may offer if the interviews were guided by the researcher. The selection of participants from the same geographical location could also limit generalization (Emerson, 2015). Generalization in case study designs results from themes and principles that emerge from participants' narratives rather than statistically derived data used in quantitative studies (Anderson & Colleagues, 2014). As a matter of fact, themes derived from participants in geographically dispersed locations differed, thereby limiting generalization.

Assumptions, Risks and Biases

Qualitative research is usually more prone to bias than quantitative research. It is easy to make some selection, interview, or measurement biases and unrealistic assumptions in qualitative research. Bias in research is one of the factors for the poor validity of research outcomes. It is a situation whereby the researcher influences the process of an investigation. It poses a huge obstacle for researchers in achieving credibility and accuracy in a study. In the study, the researcher was not involved in any act that eroded the credibility and validity of the research outcomes. It was assumed that the participants understood the effect of transformational leadership on employees' satisfaction in the United States banking sector, as they were drawn from the United States banking sector and possessed many years of working experience.

Since this research entailed a descriptive qualitative study, the researcher was more passionate about the process, meaning, and understanding gained through the interview and focus group discussions with the participants. It is also assumed that the findings of the study were more realistic since the data obtained from the participants conveyed multiple perspectives. The procedures adopted by the researcher in this study were based on the researcher's experience obtaining and analyzing data. Considering the nature of descriptive qualitative studies, the interaction between the researcher and the participants could have posed some risks to the research outcome as the researcher and the participants were personally involved in different stages of the study. These risks are anonymity, confidentiality, and informed consent. The roles of the participants were well-defined, and the use of practical guidelines in all the stages of the research was encouraged.

Confidentiality refers to a situation where the personal information of the participants should not be revealed except by their permission (Surmiak, 2018). The researcher endeavored to reduce the possibility of intrusion into the personal information of the participants by all means. The researcher also informed the participants of the different stages of the research in simple language. Anonymization is one of the forms of confidentiality, which involves concealing the participants' identities (Surmiak, 2018). Therefore, the principle of anonymity was obeyed at all times in this study.

Trustworthiness of the Research

The most important criteria used for assessing the trustworthiness of qualitative research are credibility, transferability, dependability, and conformability. The confirmability of the study was tested by using an audit trail to check the field work performed by the researcher (Patton, 2015). An audit trail in a qualitative study explains the collection of data in detail and the basis for arriving at the researcher's decisions throughout the study (Merriam & Tisdell, 2016). The purpose of this is to reduce bias and maximize accuracy with a view to reporting any impartiality during the research process. Confirmability in the study was checked by using thick, rich quotes that personify the emerging themes of the study. Dependability relates to the consistency of the data under the same conditions (Cope, 2014). Dependability can be achieved when another researcher agrees with the decision trails at each stage of the research (Cope, 2014). The researcher employed an audit trail to enhance dependability in this study. An audit trail refers to the collection of materials that are used to record the researcher's assumptions and decisions. It indicates the method of data collection and decision-making (Merriam & Tisdell, 2016).

Conformability is defined as the ability of the researcher to confirm that the data represents the participants' views (Cope, 2014). The researcher also used an audit trail to ensure the conformability of the data.

Credibility relates to the correctness of the data obtained from the participants and the researcher's interpretation and presentation of the data (Yin, 2016). A credible study assures the researcher that data has been properly collected and interpreted so that the findings and conclusions accurately reflect and represent the phenomenon of the study (Yin, 2016).

Transferability refers to the application of the findings of the study to other settings or groups (Cope, 2014). Transferability can be achieved if the qualitative study makes some sense to individuals not involved in the study and the audience can relate the results to their own experiences. To exhibit transferability within this study, the researcher provided sufficient descriptive data to make transferability possible (Merriam & Tisdell, 2016).

Significance of the Study

In today's complex business world, employee satisfaction is seen as an indispensable element to achieving organizational success and excellence (Singh, 2019). Transformational leaders establish a greater involvement in the work of subordinates, thereby making organizations attain higher efficiency and employee satisfaction (Singh, 2019). This study provided a robust understanding of how transformational leadership drove employee satisfaction. The effect of transformational leadership on employee satisfaction cannot be over-emphasized. Prior empirical studies have investigated the direct positive impact of transformational leadership on employee satisfaction but are not comprehensive enough to provide thorough evidence (Chai et al., 2017). Given this, the present study attempted to provide more theoretical and empirical evidence on the effect of transformational leadership on employee satisfaction in the United States banking sector.

Employees' satisfaction can be achieved if organizations promote transformational leadership (Chai et al., 2017). Thus, raising transformational leaders will enable the followers to derive the positive effect of transformational leadership (Chai et al., 2017). The study offered significant relevance to organizations in leadership as it identified aspects of transformational leadership that impacted employee satisfaction with their work. Furthermore, it was known from published research that Transformational leadership impacted employees' performance through the transformation of the followers who transcended beyond self-interests for the sake of organizational interest (Steinmann et al., 2018).

This research is also essential because transformational leaders commit themselves to selfless ideals with a view to aligning their values with that of their followers and the organization (Luk & Lazoo, 2020). This study also considered the main components of transformational leadership that enhance organizational employee satisfaction. These consist of idealized influence, inspirational motivation, intellectual stimulation, and individualized consideration. This research is useful in the banking sector of the United States economy because it serves as a roadmap for the analysis of the effect of transformational leadership on employee satisfaction in the banking sector of the United States economy. The banking sector of the United States economy was considered because there is no qualitatively research-oriented study that focuses on the effect of transformational leadership on employee satisfaction in the United States banking sector. Thus, this research filled the gap identified from the review of the literature.

Transformational leadership is suggested to be a key driver for business success and a better workplace experience since the interactions between the transformational leader and the followers significantly impact employees' satisfaction and, ultimately, the performance of the organization at large (Li et al., 2019). This research differs from other studies on the effect of transformational leadership on employee satisfaction because of its emphasis on the United States banking sector based on a qualitative study.

Transformational leadership can be understood as creating a vision and delivering a sense of belonging to employees (Tse, 2008). This study is relevant at both micro and macro levels, and as such, it provides a valuable guide for banks in the United States economy as well as other sectors of the United States economy. Job satisfaction is one of the most complicated areas bank managers face today when managing their employees (Abdolshah et al., 2018). The study's findings will be useful for academics and future researchers who may want to undertake research about the effect of transformational leadership on employee satisfaction. The recommendations made in this study will be beneficial to the parties mentioned above by providing empirical evidence to individuals, government entities, and corporate bodies who may want to conduct further research on the research area.

Summary

The purpose of the qualitative descriptive research is to provide robust evidence on the effect of transformational leadership on employee satisfaction in the United States banking sector. A qualitative descriptive study is appropriate for providing answers to the research question "How do bank employees describe the effect of transformational leadership on their job satisfaction?" and "How do bank employees describe the influence of collaborations between leaders and followers on employees' satisfaction?" These two questions provide answers to the effect of transformational leadership on employee satisfaction in the United States banking sector. The study utilized a descriptive qualitative research design and employed a questionnaire as the research instrument. The questionnaire was administered to 15 bank employees in the United States.

Additionally, a one-on-one interview was conducted with the same 15 participants to enhance the credibility of the study. Furthermore, 10 other participants were involved in focus group discussions to gather their responses. The selection of the 25 participants was based on purposive sampling. The study adhered to the requirements and ethical guidelines of South University Online, and measures were taken to maintain the confidentiality of the participants and protect their data.

Chapter 4: Data Analysis and Results

Introduction

This qualitative descriptive study addresses the impact of transformational leadership on job satisfaction and the influence of collaboration between leaders and followers on employees' satisfaction in the banking industry of the United States. To answer the two research questions, the researcher interviewed 25 participants via zoom video teleconferencing. Out of the 25 participants that made up the sample of this study, 15 partook in the interview, while the remaining 10 participated in focus group discussions. The participants that constituted the focus group discussions did not partake in the interview. This section addressed the two research questions of the study stated below by analyzing the data collected from participants and presenting the results based on findings from the analysis.

RQ 1: How do bank employees describe transformational leadership's impact on their job satisfaction?

RQ 2: How do bank employees describe the impact of leader-follower collaboration on employee satisfaction?

There has been no prior research on the influence of transformative leadership on employee satisfaction in the banking sector in the United States. The research will help to close this gap. The significance of this study lies in its focus on employee satisfaction, which is crucial for achieving organizational success in today's complex corporate climate (Singh, 2019).
Moreover, this study significantly impacts firms as it explores specific aspects of transformational leadership that directly affect employee satisfaction.

In line with the study's objectives, this chapter analyzed the data obtained from the descriptive qualitative study, presenting and interpreting the results. The study specifically investigated the impact of transformational leadership on employees' satisfaction and also examined the influence of collaboration between leaders and followers on employee satisfaction. To collect the necessary data, the researcher employed semi-structured interviews and conducted focus group discussions. The study adopted a descriptive qualitative research design and a well- defined data management plan to ensure proper organization and storage of the collected information. Collected data from the interview and focus group discussion were cleaned by removing duplicates, correcting typos on and inconsistencies in the transcripts. To analyze the data, the researcher implemented Saldana's coding and theming method, which facilitated the identification of key reporting themes. The study's findings revealed that transformational leadership plays a significant role in shaping job satisfaction and overall employee satisfaction within the banking sector in the United States. The findings of this chapter, which will also serve as a basis for drawing reasonable conclusions and recommendations, are further elaborated in Chapter Five. Chapter Five provides a comprehensive summary of the study, including a summary of the findings, conclusion, recommendations, implications of the study, and suggestions for further studies.

Prior to engaging participants in interviews and focus groups, a robust process of obtaining informed consent was meticulously followed. This process entailed providing participants with comprehensive information about the study's objectives, procedures, potential benefits, and any associated risks. Participants were given the opportunity to ask questions and seek clarification before voluntarily agreeing to participate. The informed consent process was designed to empower participants with the knowledge they needed to make an informed decision about their involvement, ensuring their autonomy and willingness to share their experiences candidly. The informed consent was sent to selected participants via email through Respondents. Participants reverted indicating their acceptance to the process as clearly stated in the informed consent.

Data Analysis

Preparation of Raw Data

Interviews and focus group discussions were used to collect the information used for this study. The researcher did not create a separate demographic questionnaire for the study, but Respondents, an online survey company, was able to collect the participants' demographic information. The recruitment template (Appendix G) and informed consent (Appendix C) were also mailed to the online survey company (Respondents) for the recruitment of participants.

Fifteen candidates were vetted for the interview, while 10 were screened for the focus group discussion. The screening was based on the following inclusion criteria of this study: a minimum of 10 years of experience in the banking sector, a minimum of Associate Degree/Bachelor of Science or its equivalent, and an age range of 30 to 45 years (Appendix A). Participants with Bachelor of Arts were also considered in the study since it was an equivalent of Bachelor of Science. Data cleansing is an essential component of qualitative research because it ensures the quality and validity of the data and enables the researcher to draw meaningful and accurate conclusions from the analysis (Bhandari, 2022). The process involves identifying and correcting spelling and grammatical errors, removing words commonly used in informal speech but not for formal reports, comparing the accuracy of the transcribed text to the audio or video recording of the interview, and ensuring that all pertinent data was captured. This procedure is designed to improve the data's reliability and validity by ensuring it is as accurate and comprehensive as feasible.

Although data cleansing is recognized as an initial or preprocessing step in the knowledge discovery in the databases process (Brachman & Anand, 1996; Fayyad et al., 1996), no specific definition or perspective is provided for the data cleansing process (Maletic & Marcus, 2005). The data cleansing process is associated with data acquisition and definition, or it can be utilized to enhance data quality in an existing system. The data cleansing process comprises three phases: defining and identifying error types, searching for and detecting error instances, and rectifying the identified errors. This process presents a complex problem, and a diverse range of specialized methods and technologies can be employed for each phase. (Maletic & Marcus, 2005).

In order to improve the integrity of the data, the researcher conducted a process of data cleansing, wherein the interview transcripts were thoroughly examined, and any instances of data inconsistencies and transcription errors were identified and subsequently eliminated. During the data cleaning procedure, the researcher eliminated 21 errors resulting from slips of the tongue, 18 errors resulting from incorrect punctuation, and 46 errors resulting from transcription errors.

Data cleansing is a crucial phase in analyzing qualitative data, particularly interview transcripts (Bhandari, 2022). The online survey agency (Respondents) obtained the demographic information of the participants based on the inclusion criteria established by the researcher and sent to the company (Respondents). The information is provided in Appendix A - Interview Protocol/Inclusion Criteria.

Descriptive Findings

Table 1 below presents detailed demographic characteristics participants that participated in the interview and focus group discussion. The demography shows their gender distribution, highest educational qualification, years of experience and participants age distribution.

Table 1

Demographic Background of the Participants

Items			Total
Interview participants Gender	Male: 11	Female: 4	15
Focus group participants Gender	Male: 7	Female: 3	10
Qualification	AS/BSC: 19	MASTERS: 6	25
Working Experience	10-15 Years: 21	16-20 Years: 4	25
Age	30-38 Years: 16	39-45 Years: 9	25

Table 2 presents the interview duration for each of the 15 participants and 2 focus groups, along with the corresponding transcript sizes. It highlights that the interviews had an average duration of 58 minutes and 13 seconds, resulting in transcripts spanning an average of 7 pages. In comparison, the average time for focus group discussions was 66 minutes and 1 second, producing transcripts spanning an average of 10 pages.

Table 2

Table Showing Interview/Focus group Time Average group, and Transcriptions Data

Identifier	Time: Min: Sec	Pages Transcribed (single space)
Interview		
P1	47:04	7
P2	55:19	6
P3	54:06	7
P4	50:35	7
P5	68:27	6
P6	62:11	8
P7	50:40	6
P8	71:08	7
P9	83:12	8
P10	51:13	6
P11	49:05	6
P12	55:29	8
P13	68:56	9
P14	52:17	6
P15	52:18	6
AVERAGE	58:13	7
Focus Group		
FG1	55:41	9
F1		
F2		
F3		
F4		
F5		
FG2	76:20	10
F6		
F7		
F8		
F9		
F10P25		
AVERAGE	66.01	10

Data Analysis Procedures

Thematic analysis was used to characterize the characteristics of the content of the interviews and focus group discussions by identifying, examining, and analyzing the themes within the collected data. Version 12 of the qualitative data management software MaxQDA version 12 was used for the classification process.

According to Saldana (2016), a theme is not simply a coded entity but rather the result of coding, categorization, and analytical reflection. The Saldana method of coding and theming was utilized to characterize the characteristics of the content of the interviews and focus group discussions by identifying, examining, and analyzing the reporting themes within the gathered data. Beginning with the accumulation of data and concluding with the answering and interpretation of research questions, the research focused on the themes surrounding the two questions listed above.

According to Saldana's approach, there are six stages involved in qualitative research thematic analysis. Thematic analysis is a method in which the researcher identifies, analyzes, and reports patterns or themes in a study. This Saldana thematic analysis method includes becoming acquainted with the data, generating initial codes, searching for themes, reviewing themes, naming, defining, and reporting themes (Saldana, 2016).

The researcher analyzed the semi-structured interviews and focus group discussions using open coding, axial coding, and thematic analysis. The interview and focus group inquiries are centered on the two primary research questions, and transcripts of the interviews and focus group discussions were uploaded to MaxQDA.version12. The researcher investigated the collected data critically to identify and highlight common themes and repeated phrases. Additionally, the researcher evaluated the data multiple times to distinguish unique codes from a vast array of similar codes.

The first step in data analysis is the identification of themes. The responses of the participants disclosed repeated codes and themes. The data were organized by identifying individual codes, characterizing the codes, and determining the frequency with which a code occurs. The researcher examined the credibility of the codes by comparing the collected data to the research questions and then extracted themes from the codes. It is important to note that the coding process was coupled with the thematic analysis. The researcher verifies that the data has been evaluated for the identified codes to correspond with the research questions. The procedures involved in data analysis include the researcher's administration of interviews and focus group discussions via Zoom video teleconferencing, the transcription of interviews and focus group discussions using MAXQDA software version 12, and the verification of the transcripts by members.

The researcher took important notes during the interviews and focus group discussions to ensure the transcriptions were accurate. Member verification of the transcripts increased the reliability of the collected data. By uploading the transcripts into MAXQDA version 12, the researcher also created codes and devised a few themes. To enhance the credibility of the transcriptions, the researcher assessed the keywords and phrases. The researcher reviewed, reorganized, and redefined themes and compared them to the collected data to ensure the themes addressed the research questions.

In addition, the following steps were taken to ensure that the transcripts were properly coded: the transcription of the data obtained through the interviews and focus group discussions using MaxQDA, the researcher's use of the color coding feature to identify keywords, solitary words, phrases, and sentences used by the participants, the repeated review of the transcripts to verify the accuracy of the identified codes from the transcripts, and the identification of the most frequently occurring codes. For the research, a paper trail is used; a paper trail is the accumulation of documents used to document the researcher's assumptions and decisions. It specifies the data acquisition and decision-making methodology (Merriam & Tisdell, 2016). The researcher utilized an audit trail to ensure data conformity (Appendix G). The collection and analysis of data went according to plan. Still, data collection encountered two obstacles: the unavailability of some participants and the inability of others to answer the specified research questions. Respondents, an online survey company, substituted original participants who were unavailable or unable are unavailable or unable to answer research questions with new participants, so these obstacles will not impact the study's outcome. Currently, there is no difference between Chapters 3 and 4.

In order to disclose codes, categories, and themes within collected data, the axial coding technique was used to link data together. Axial coding is a qualitative method for analyzing data and identifying relationships between categories and subcategories (Simmons, 2022). It entails the identification of codes, which are labels or tags assigned to particular data items, followed by the categorization of these codes into larger groups. In axial coding, the researcher establishes connections between codes, identifies which codes from open coding are the most significant and central to your theory, and elevates them to category status. In qualitative research using axial coding, you examine the codes and their underlying data to determine how they can be grouped and abstracted into categories. These categories could be developed by abstracting an existing code or creating new concepts encompassing multiple codes. These are the "axes" that their supporting algorithms revolve around. Then, themes are derived from related categories.

The codes extracted from the transcripts are presented in Appendix H - Coding of transcribed documents. The table visually represents the research analysis codes as exported from MAXQDA version 12. Each code was represented by a unique color code, making distinguishing between the various codes simpler. The table also includes the number of segments where each code appears and the number of documents containing each code. The table displays, for each of the 17 transcribed documents, the number of instances where each code appeared. This information would help determine which data codes were more prevalent and which were less prevalent. Overall, the table extracted from MAXQDA version 12 software is a useful tool for organizing and analyzing data, as it enables simple identification and comparison of the various codes and their frequency across the transcribed documents.

The extracted codes were coalesced into categories (Appendix I - Coding to Categories). The researcher discovered that some of the detected codes were redundant or closely related. To simplify the analysis and obtain a better understanding of the data, the researcher renamed and merged these similar codes into larger categories. This allowed the researcher to identify 17 distinct categories. These categories are the main "axes" around which the supporting codes were organized, and they provide a clear framework for analyzing and interpreting the data. By categorizing the codes, the researchers were able to make a more systematic and structured sense of the data and identify patterns and relationships that may not have been immediately apparent.

Data analysis in qualitative research entails identifying patterns and themes within the collected data (Delve & Limpaecher, 2020). Researchers utilized axial coding techniques to organize data into categories, which were then grouped into themes. Appendix I presents the initial categories derived from the data, which were then merged into six themes that corresponded to the study's research questions, see Appendix J. By categorizing the categories into themes, the researcher was able to obtain a deeper understanding of the data's overall patterns and relationships. This process also permitted the researcher to address the research questions more directly.

In qualitative research, organizing the data into main themes is a common technique (Caulfield, 2019). This approach helped to provide the analysis with a distinct structure and framework. The researcher can identify patterns, draw conclusions, and make recommendations based on the data by grouping related categories into themes. Categorizing data into themes requires careful consideration and interpretation of the data and iterative analysis to refine and revise the themes until they accurately represent the key concepts and patterns within the data.

Results

This qualitative descriptive study investigates the influence of transformational leadership on job satisfaction and how collaborations between leaders and followers affect employee satisfaction in the United States banking sector. This study's findings are presented in a narrative format that is objective, non-evaluative, and organized by research questions. The researcher used inductive thematic analysis to determine the codes, categories, and themes. This process formed six themes that align with the study's research questions. Three of the themes align with the first research question. In contrast, the remaining three themes align with the second research question.

Results for Supporting Research Question 1

The research question sets out how bank employees describe the influence of transformational leadership on their job satisfaction. The three themes linked with this research question were derived from like categories that were also coalesced from related codes using the axial technique. This section describes each theme's analysis and relates them to research question one. It also described the process of creating each theme from the respective codes and categories.

Table 3

Analysis of Themes 1, 2 and 3

Research Question	Themes
How do bank employees describe the influence of transformational leadership on their job satisfaction?	Theme 1: Transformational leadership enhances performance
	Theme 2: Transformational leadership influences employee loyalty
	Theme 3: Transformational leadership result to desired outcome

Although all three themes align with research question one, theme one Transformational leadership enhances performance, is more significant because it has the highest frequency of codes 626 that formed theme one. This is followed by theme three, Transformational leadership result to desired outcome, with 260 codes frequency, then theme two, Transformational leadership influence employee loyalty, with 170 codes frequency. The method by which each theme was derived from the respective codes are described below and the themes were analyzed in relation to the first research question.

Table 4

Transformational leadership and performance according to Theme 1

Codes	Categories	Theme
Practice		
Adoption		
Growth	Organization Performance	
Openness		
Drive profit		
Transformational		
Performance		
Employees	Employees' performance	
Perform		Transformational leadership enhances performance
Engag		
Vision		
Trust		
Common value	Organization vision	
Teammates		
Folks		
Goal		
Set goal	Shared vision	
Common goal		
Leadership		

Theme 1: Transformational Leadership Enhances Performance in Relation to Job Satisfaction

The first theme that emerged from the data analysis was transformational leadership enhances performance. The theme "Transformational leadership influence performance in relation to job satisfaction" was selected because it directly addresses research question one regarding the influence of transformational leadership on job satisfaction among bank employees. This theme explores how transformational leadership impacts employee performance in the banking industry. By examining the association between transformational leadership and performance, valuable insights were gained into how leadership style affects employee satisfaction and overall job experiences. The theme emerged from coalescing 19 codes into four subthemes: organizational performance, employee performance, organizational vision, and shared vision. The organization performance subtheme was created by combining the following codes: practice, adoption, growth, openness, profit-driving, and transformational. Employees' performance subtheme was created by combining the following codes: performance, employees, perform, and engage. The organization's vision subtheme was created by merging vision, trust, common values, teammates, and folks. While coalescing goals, set goals, common goals, and leadership formed the shared vision subtheme. Thematic analysis of the participant responses revealed that transformational leadership enhanced the performance of banks in the United States. Most participants emphasized that transformational leadership involves a shared vision that enhances employee and organizational performance.

Organizational performance

Transformational leadership plays a crucial role in influencing organizational performance, which, in turn, can lead to increased employee job satisfaction. This relationship stems from the transformative and inspiring nature of this leadership style, which can positively impact various aspects of an organization's functioning. Transformational leadership's emphasis on vision, motivation, support, empowerment, and organizational excellence creates an environment conducive to higher organizational performance. The positive influence of transformational leadership on organizational performance creates a ripple effect that enhances employee job satisfaction and overall organizational well-being.

As expressed by P1, transformational leadership is believed to enhance performance, and this belief is not limited to P1's personal opinion but is also shared by colleagues within the office. The reference to collective agreement implies that there is a consensus among office members that transformational leadership positively contributes to overall organizational performance. The recognition of this shared opinion among colleagues further reinforces the argument that transformational leadership is widely acknowledged as a significant factor in organizational performance. The presence of this belief among multiple individuals within the organization indicates a broader understanding and acceptance of the positive impact of transformational leadership.

According to P7, transformational leaders play a crucial role in creating an environment where employees feel motivated and engaged to work towards shared goals. The perception that leaders are putting in lots of effort is a powerful example for employees, motivating them to contribute their best efforts. When leaders are seen as active participants in achieving organizational goals, it fosters a sense of shared responsibility and dedication throughout the organization. Transformational leaders often inspire and motivate employees by setting high expectations, providing support and guidance, and encouraging individual growth and development. The recognition of transformational leadership's positive influence on performance by both P1 and P7 suggests that it significantly enhances overall organizational performance.

The collective agreement among colleagues and the observation of leaders' active involvement in achieving goals indicate that transformational leadership fosters a collective effort, commitment, and dedication to achieving organizational success.

Employee's performance

Transformational leadership has a direct impact on employees' performance, which in turn can lead to higher levels of employee job satisfaction. This relationship is grounded in the transformative and empowering nature of this leadership style, which enhances various aspects of employees' work experiences and outcomes. According to P2 and P9, Transformational leadership improves confidence and encourages employees to perform better. This suggests that transformational leaders inspire and empower employees, enabling them to perform better in their roles. When asked how transformational leadership affects performance, P15 stated, "Transformational leadership helps me manage the people under me. It does impact my performance. It instills confidence and coaching skills in me. It impacts my performance because I am trusted with my tasks." They submit that effective people management can improve team morale, productivity, and performance. By developing coaching skills, individuals can better guide and support their team members, leading to better outcomes for the organization. Furthermore, feeling trusted with tasks can increase an individual's sense of responsibility and accountability, motivating them to perform to the best of their abilities.

Organizational vision

P3 and P11 highlighted the importance of having a clear vision and communicating. According to P11, transformational leadership plays a role in aligning employees with the organizational vision and fostering employee engagement and buy-in. Additionally, it was noted by P4 that regular meetings are held to deliberate on the vision and goals of the organization.

This suggests that transformational leadership plays a role in promoting effective communication and the widespread dissemination of the vision among all members of the organization.

Furthermore, P4 stated that transformational leaders have a clear and compelling vision of what the bank can accomplish, and they communicate this vision to their employees in a manner that inspires and motivates them to work towards it. According to P2, transformational leadership provides the training necessary to comprehend and learn how to drive the business, thereby positively influencing the bank's shared vision. They reiterated that when employees receive training and development opportunities, they can better comprehend the bank's goals and objectives and how to accomplish them. This can result in increased productivity, enhanced performance, and a more committed workforce.

Shared vision

P1 and P3 stated that transformational leadership improves employee communication and engagement, leading to a better understanding and shared commitment to organizational goals. P3 also posits that transformational leadership enhances the organization's clarity and visibility of shared goals. P7 stated, "People here are working towards the same goal; even though we may have different positions work in different areas, we're all working for the benefit of the bank, and we realize that our leaders are putting in as much work or more work than we are".

In their statement, they highlighted the importance of a shared vision and a sense of purpose within an organization. When all employees understand and work towards a common goal, it can lead to increased collaboration, teamwork, and a sense of unity. Furthermore, when employees recognize the efforts of their leaders, it can lead to a more positive work culture and increased trust in leadership. F3 said, "It is important all departments be on the same page and efficiently communicate; it impacts the customer experience and organizational success."

According to P11, having that goal or the vision on display, having it known, definitely plays a big part in getting there and employee engagement and buy-in. They submitted that displaying goals and vision can also increase transparency and accountability within the bank. Employees are more likely to understand what is expected of them and what they are working towards, which can lead to increased motivation and engagement.

Table 5

Transformational leadership influences employee loyalty according to Theme 2

Codes	Categories	Theme
Satisfaction Motivation Promotion	Employees' satisfaction	
Loyal Anniversary Retire Happy Honesty Confidence Value	Employee Loyalty	Transformational leadership influences employee loyalty

Theme 2: Transformational Leadership Influences Employee Loyalty

The second theme emerged as transformational leadership's influence on employee loyalty. Theme 2 was selected because it directly aligns with your research question one: the influence of transformational leadership on job satisfaction among bank employees. This theme explores the effect of transformational leadership on employee loyalty within the banking industry. By selecting this theme, the researchers were able to investigate how transformational leaders inspire loyalty among their employees through their leadership behaviors and practices. The theme provided insights into transformational leaders' specific behaviors and actions that contribute to employee loyalty, such as providing mentorship, empowering employees, and promoting personal and professional development. By selecting this theme, valuable data were gathered that directly address the research question and provide insights into the effect of transformational leadership on employee loyalty and job satisfaction in the banking sector. The theme emerged by combining two subthemes employee satisfaction and employee loyalty.

Employee satisfaction was derived by combining the codes, satisfaction, motivation, and promotion, whereas employee loyalty was derived by combining seven codes: loyalty, anniversary, retire, joyful, honesty, confidence, and value. This theme explains transformational leadership's impact on employee satisfaction and loyalty.

Employee satisfaction

The subtheme of employee satisfaction emerges from the participants' responses. P11 mentioned that the overall culture and work-life balance at their organization contribute to employee satisfaction, resulting from transformational leadership. Additionally, participants P2, P3, P4, P6, P13, P15, and F3 discussed the impact of transformational leadership on their day-today work and highlighted elements such as autonomy, freedom to develop their job, and effective communication as factors contributing to their job satisfaction. P9, in his submission, said employees found solutions to any challenging task within their peers because they all share a mutual objective of achieving success which makes them fulfilled. His statement reads,

> It can be challenging sometimes, but ultimately, we all have a requirement in our job, you know, the big bosses, they give out what they look for and what they want, and then we have to communicate that to our peers, alright?
>
> Getting the tasks done in such form encourages employees.

During the second focus group session, F6 shared a perspective that resonated with other participants. According to them, transformational leadership promotes active involvement and communication with fellow peers and managers to ensure that tasks are completed smoothly and efficiently. This approach fosters a collaborative work environment where everyone can contribute their ideas and perspectives towards achieving a common goal and getting satisfaction from the job.

According to P7, the utilization of a transformational leadership style facilitates the development of robust interpersonal connections within a team. This, in turn, leads to increased levels of satisfaction and productivity. They stated,

> "My role specifically having that ability to kind of work independently and tap me on the shoulder. If I need engagement's help is more or less the way things work in my world and that helps me get a lot more done."

P4 also stated that giving people the freedom to try and develop their jobs is the best. They get the task done in their best way and are always satisfied doing it. The absence of micromanagement in work environment was expressed and appreciated by F3, who stated,

Really, it's nice to not be micromanage and have some and breathing down your neck all the time. It just makes me kind of a more effective, employing Junior Banker when I'm able to manage processes and utilize resources as needed.

According to P6, transformational leadership gives opportunity to increase work output and also learn new ways of doing things logically.

Employee loyalty

Most employees at P4's bank chose to retire, indicating their loyalty to the bank and reluctance to leave. This observation highlights how transformational leadership played a role in enhancing employees' loyalty to the bank. P6 believes that transformational leaders can strengthen employees' connection to the organization and their intent to remain by creating a supportive work environment, providing opportunities for growth and development, and fostering a shared purpose. The viewpoint of F10 differs regarding bank loyalty. They believe that many banks failed to exercise transformational leadership effectively and instead prioritize sales, thereby negatively impacting the loyalty of employees. However, members of focus group 2, including F6, F7, F8, and F9, disagree with F10. They feel loyal to their institutions as a result of the utilized transformational leadership style.

It was acknowledged by P3 that there were other employment opportunities available in other banks that had the potential to offer higher financial rewards. However, they expressed their decision to stay at his current bank, citing career development as the primary reason. "The less likely an employee abandons a bank, the greater their loyalty to it," stated P3. The participants disclosed that employee loyalty is one benefit of transformational leadership, and when employees are comfortable with the bank's leadership style, they do not consider changing jobs.

Transformational leadership fosters loyalty and enthusiasm among employees, leading to a strong desire to remain on the job for an extended period (F1). They emphasized the enjoyment derived from the continuous learning experience of transformational leadership. In his submission, P7 stated, "I have to say I've never really been as loyal to any other place that I've worked until this one. This one far surpasses it because they make me feel important; they make me feel part of a team like I'm part of something bigger."

According to P8, a competent and effective leadership team is vital in cultivating an atmosphere of growth within the organization. This positive environment ensures that employees do not feel compelled to seek opportunities elsewhere and are motivated to stay and develop their careers within the organization. This indicates that effective leadership contributes to employee satisfaction and fosters a sense of professional development, an increased workload, and improved salary and benefits. P11 highlighted the long tenure of employees at Discover, with some having worked for the company for 10, 15, 25, or even 30 years. They attributed this loyalty to the culture established by Discover, which emphasizes work-life balance, a strong benefit program, and transformational leadership. The overall culture drives engagement and employee satisfaction, thereby creating an environment where employees choose to stay for extended periods. F9 also expressed a long-term commitment to the bank, having worked there for over 20 years. They attributed their loyalty to the bank's transformational mindset, where leaders prioritize associates' well-being, treat them as professionals, and avoid micromanagement. This approach fosters employee satisfaction and loyalty.

Table 6

Transformational leadership result to desired outcome according to Theme 3

Codes	Categories	Theme
Outcome Output Success	Desired Outcome	
Better Result	Best Result	
Role Job Responsibilities Interference Feedback Role	Assign tasks	Transformational leadership result to desired outcome
Coaching Strategy Training	Leadership support	

Theme 3: Transformational Leadership Result to Desired Outcome

Theme 3, Transformational leadership result to desired outcome, was chosen due to its distinct viewpoint on the impact of transformational leadership on job satisfaction in the banking sector. The selection of this theme facilitated the exploration of how transformational leaders inspire and motivate their employees to exceed expectations, resulting in favorable outcomes such as enhanced productivity, improved performance, and successful goal achievement. This theme emerged from combining two subthemes: "desired outcome" and "best outcome." The subtheme "desired outcome" was formed by integrating three codes: outcome, output, and success, while "best outcome" was created by merging two codes: better and result. This theme emphasized the importance of transformational leadership in achieving an organization's desired outcome. Most participants emphasized that transformational leadership positively affects the bank's intended outcome.

Desired outcome

Transformational leadership positively influences the organization when embraced with a sincere desire to learn and grow (P1). This leadership style promotes a positive working environment and enhances the organization's understanding of its customers. Transformational leadership encourages continuous learning and growth, contributing to a more harmonious and customer-centric workplace and aligning with the organization's desired outcome of continuous learning and growth. According to P3, the transparency aspect of transformational leadership has played a crucial role in motivating employees to give their best effort. Their statement reads, "Therefore, I believe that because they are so transparent, they influence you to do your best and achieve more." Leaders create an environment of trust and authenticity by being open and honest with employees, which, in turn, fosters a sense of commitment and dedication among the employees, enabling them to work towards the accomplishment of the bank's mission and vision. The transparency aspect of transformational leadership helps align the employees' efforts with the organization's overall goals, leading to increased success and achievement.

According to P15, their bank achieves the desired outcome through its superiors' continuous evaluation and review process. By conducting regular assessments of senior leadership, including the CEO, the bank ensures that the performance of these leaders is closely monitored and assessed. This evaluation process allows for feedback and provides an opportunity for improvement. The bank creates a continuous improvement and development culture by holding its leaders accountable and providing written feedback. This commitment to evaluating and reviewing superiors contributes to achieving the intended outcomes and helps drive the transformational leadership approach within the organization. It could also encourage regular communication between employees and their superiors to maintain clarity regarding goals, objectives, and expectations and resolve any issues or challenges that may arise during work. The superiors could also provide employees with assistance, direction, and mentoring, enhancing their skills, knowledge, and performance. The participant stated, "Intriguingly, our company conducts reviews on all of its senior leadership, so we are essentially evaluating our CEO and providing feedback." Our chief risk officer will provide written feedback on them.
Therefore, I believe that gets empowering for us because, without transformation and all of that, a company cannot develop."

P9 expressed that transformational leadership serves as a way to align peers and ensure consistent practices, reflecting the desired outcome of fostering unity, cohesion, and standardized approaches within the organization. Additionally, P11 emphasized the positive impact of transformational leadership on productivity and overall company success, with the desired outcome being to drive employee performance and ultimately benefit the organization.

The transparency exhibited by transformational leaders significantly impacts individuals, motivating them to strive for their best and achieve more (P3). By being open and honest in their communication, transformational leaders create an environment where employees feel valued and included, fostering trust and encouraging individuals to put forth their best effort. This transparency also ensures their contributions are recognized and appreciated, motivating them to exceed expectations and reach higher performance levels. In essence, transformational leadership encourages individuals to reach their full potential, aligning with the desired outcome of maximizing individual performance. Their statement reads, "Therefore, I believe that because they are so transparent, they influence you to do your best and achieve more." P7 emphasized the importance placed by their bank on diversity, equity, and inclusion, recognizing the benefits of a diverse workforce. This indicates that transformational leadership aims for a diverse makeup of the organization as a positive outcome. Furthermore, P8 described the desired outcome of developing talent within the organization, both internally within teams and externally, in serving customers and clients. Implementing a program to enhance the knowledge and skills of employees has resulted in valuable contributions and increased effectiveness.

Results for Supporting Research Question 2

To answer Research Question 2, the researcher studied how bank employees describe the influence of collaborations between leaders and followers on employee satisfaction. The study aims to address this question by investigating eight interview questions. From the research question, three overarching themes emerge to depict the influence of collaboration between leaders and followers on employee satisfaction. These themes include collaboration and employees' satisfaction, collaboration for best results, and effective leadership. The formation process of these themes and the analysis of each theme are discussed in this section

Table 7

Analysis of Themes 4, 5, and 6

Research Question	Themes
How do bank employees describe the influence of collaborations between leaders and followers on employee satisfaction?	Theme 4: Collaboration and employees' satisfaction
	Theme 5: Collaboration and best results
	Theme 6: Collaboration and effective leadership

Although all three themes align with the second research question, theme 6, "Collaboration and effective leadership," has the highest frequency of codes that formed theme one (296). It is followed by theme 5, "Collaboration and best results" (134), while theme 4, "Collaboration and employees' satisfaction," has the least code frequency (132). The method by which each theme was derived from the respective codes is discussed below, and the themes were analyzed in accordance with research question two. Table 8

Collaboration and employees' satisfaction according to Theme 4

Codes	Categories	Theme
Sense of belonging		
Satisfaction	Employees' steadfastness	
Salary		
Express		
Collaborator	Followers' satisfaction	
Review		Collaboration and employees'
Synerg		
Interaction		
Mutual exchange of ideas	Followers' performance	
Work together		

Theme 4: Collaboration and Employees' Satisfaction

The fourth theme emerged from three categories: employee steadfastness, followers' satisfaction, and followers' performance. Theme 4 was selected as it directly addressed research question 2, which focused on how bank employees perceive the influence of collaborations between leaders and followers on their workplace satisfaction. The theme explored the dynamics of collaboration, particularly between leaders and followers, and its impact on employee satisfaction. By choosing this theme, the researcher had the opportunity to delve into bank employees' experiences, perspectives, and feedback regarding their collaborative interactions with their leaders.

The combination of ten codes led to the creation of these categories. Employee steadfastness was formed by combining four codes: a sense of belonging, satisfaction, salary, and expression. Followers' satisfaction was derived from three codes: collaborator, review, and synergy. Similarly, followers' performance was created by combining three codes: interaction, mutual exchange of ideas, and working together. This theme provides insight into the relationship between collaboration and employees' satisfaction and performance.

Employees' steadfastness

Most respondents believe collaboration between the leader and the followers increases employee motivation and satisfaction. P2 believes that employee collaboration can have a positive effect on job satisfaction. When employees are encouraged to collaborate and share ideas, they perceive that their contributions are valued by their coworkers and the organization. This sense of recognition and appreciation can be a potent motivator for employees, fostering a sense of dedication and loyalty to the organization. They stated,

> I have no doubt that collaboration can impact employee satisfaction, as I believe it stems from an employee's perception of their value and the importance of their input. When it comes down to it, regardless of your position, you want to feel appreciated.

When employees feel valued through collaboration with their colleagues, they are likelier to extend that feeling to their managers and supervisors (P3). P1 emphasized that increased involvement and open communication at all levels of the organization leads to better satisfaction among workers. When employees feel valued and their talents are acknowledged, they develop a sense of belonging and perceive themselves as integral parts of the organization.

The influence of a better manager or leader on the overall work experience was expressed by F6. They emphasized that working under a competent and effective leader can significantly improve the quality of work and job satisfaction. To create a more enjoyable work environment, a good manager or leader must possess the necessary skills and qualities to guide and support their team members, provide clear direction, offer constructive feedback, and foster a positive atmosphere. Employees can experience a workplace characterized by effective communication, support, and recognition with a positive leadership style emphasizing support and effective guidance. When leaders understand their employees' needs and provide the necessary support, it significantly enhances the overall work experience, leading to a more fulfilling professional journey. P8 emphasized that everyone possesses a creative side, and when their voices are heard and appreciated, it creates an environment where individuals can succeed and thrive in their respective roles. This suggests that transformational leadership, which values and encourages individual contributions, can unlock the creative potential of employees and lead to their success.

Followers' satisfaction

Transformational leadership significantly influences overall results, employee engagement, and satisfaction (P11). They recognized that when leaders adopt a transformational leadership style, working closely with employees and gaining their buy-in, it creates a positive influence that extends to the outcomes achieved by the organization. By building rapport, trust, and collaboration with team members, transformational leaders foster an environment where employees feel valued, motivated, and empowered to perform at their best. Working closely with agents and establishing trust contributes to creating a positive work environment that fosters satisfaction among followers. F2 highlighted the significance of feeling interested and being listened to on the job, as employees who perceive a direct correlation between their input and positive outcomes experience higher job satisfaction. The concept of social capital, emphasized by F7, underscores the importance of strong relationships with managers, and collaborative relationships fostered by transformational leadership contribute to employee satisfaction. According to F10, collaboration also contributes to greater satisfaction with the organization's leadership style, which can foster greater organizational loyalty. Their statement reads,

> I believe there is a factor involved if you feel valued as an employee. You are still going to be a more productive employee if you feel that your leadership cares about what you have to say, but again, actions speak a lot louder than words.

Followers' performance

Regarding collaboration, the participants emphasized the significance of a positive working relationship between leaders and their adherents. Collaboration is about working together to achieve a common objective and fostering a culture of trust, respect, and open communication. According to most participants, leaders must actively establish and sustain positive relationships with their subordinates for collaboration to be effective. This entails taking the time to comprehend their followers' strengths, weaknesses, and perspectives and fostering an environment where they feel secure sharing their thoughts and opinions. P2 stated, "Over the years, I've observed that when there is collaboration between leaders and followers, your performance is rated higher than if you had not collaborated; therefore, it can have a positive effect on your performance."

According to P6, collaboration and teamwork positively affect followers' performance. They emphasized that when individuals join forces, leveraging their strengths and working together, it results in enhanced performance and outcomes. Their statement reads,

> I believe it promotes positivity if it is effective. Yes, that is a positive attitude. Everyone desires to do his best. It also improves cooperation; I know that you always work together to accomplish your objectives. If one hand is down, I will go and assist the other hand in completing the task because, at the end of the day, our goals are the same. When the company achieves success, you will all receive recognition.

By leveraging team members' diverse skills, knowledge, and perspectives, collective efforts result in a more effective and efficient work process. P6 highlighted the importance of collaboration in enhancing performance, as it allows for sharing ideas, learning from one another, and finding innovative solutions to challenges. This perspective aligns with the belief that when individuals collaborate and work together towards a common goal, the combined efforts lead to greater success and overall performance improvement

F1 to F10 shared the same opinion regarding the impact of collaboration on followers' performance, and everyone concurred that collaboration has a positive effect. According to F3, if "you're willing to collaborate with management, then your employees will work harder for you, as a manager, and want to make those goals a reality, because you're trusted by the management staff." F8 added, "I don't believe collaboration is effective until the appropriate resources are in place." Effective communication, time management, and prioritization. Effective communication, time management, and prioritization are crucial for optimal performance. When these tasks are accomplished and collaborative efforts with managers and team members are established, the result will positively impact performance.

The significance of collaboration in ensuring the smooth functioning of tasks and overcoming challenges was emphasized by P4. They highlighted that by working together and fostering a collaborative environment, leadership and team members can effectively address and resolve issues that arise. P4 acknowledged that occasional hiccups may occur but can be handled and managed more effectively through collaboration. The viewpoint suggests that collaboration plays a vital role in promoting coordination, communication, and cooperation among team members, ultimately leading to the efficient and successful completion of tasks. By leveraging individuals' collective expertise and efforts, collaboration enables a proactive approach to problem-solving and ensures that operations run smoothly despite challenges.

P14 discussed the critical role of collaboration in their organization. They highlighted the importance of receiving feedback from various sources, including supervisors, peers, and individuals at different levels within the organization. This comprehensive feedback helps evaluate performance and determine the extent to which collaboration is valued and considered in the organization. The participant also mentioned the evaluation process and whether collaboration is seen as a skill or value within the bank

Table 9
Collaboration and best results according to Theme 5

Codes	Categories	Theme
Result	Best result	
Positive		
Suggesting		
Partnering	Better collaboration	Collaboration and best results
Support		
Communicate		
Teamwork		

Theme 5: Collaboration and Best Results in Terms of Employee Satisfaction

Theme 5, collaboration and best result was derived from two categories: best outcome and better collaboration. Theme 5 was selected because it directly aligns with your research question two on how bank employees describe the influence of such collaborations on their satisfaction. This theme explores the influence of collaborations on job satisfaction, which is the central focus of the research question. By selecting this theme, the researchers investigated how collaborative efforts between leaders and followers yield the best results and overall job experience. Combining a total of seven codes produced these categories. Best Result was formed by combining three codes: result, positive, and suggesting, while Better Collaboration was created by combining four codes: partnership, support, communication, and collaboration. This theme describes how collaboration can be utilized to obtain optimal results. Most respondents indicated collaboration refers to cooperation, and collaboration between the leader and the followers will foster synergy, thus achieving the best outcomes.

Best outcome

> According to F3, collaboration allows individuals to freely share their opinions and ideas.

When collaboration is encouraged and valued within a team or organization, it creates an environment where individuals feel empowered to express their thoughts and contribute their unique perspectives. This open exchange of ideas fosters a sense of excitement and interest in the work being done. F3 believes that when opinions are valued and actively sought, employees are motivated to do their best and strive for the best possible outcomes. The viewpoint suggests that collaboration facilitates effective teamwork and enhances individual engagement and commitment to achieving optimal results. P12 also acknowledged the importance of collaboration with leaders in achieving better results. Recognizing the value of collaborative efforts with leaders implies that working closely with leaders and leveraging their guidance and expertise contributes to improved outcomes and overall success. P1 stated, "Through collaboration, ideas are shared, traded, discussed, and debated." This is done in an open format where everyone's input is valued. Such an environment fosters conversation to reach a conclusion or settle on a strategy. A flatter structure promotes less hierarchy and more collaboration

Better collaboration

Collaborating with leaders can offer individuals valuable benefits such as access to expertise, networking opportunities, and valuable resources (P4). When individuals engage in collaborative efforts with their leaders, they can tap into the knowledge and experience of those in leadership positions. He stated, "I believe the best results are achieved through the collaboration of the team and its leadership." Access to expertise can help individuals enhance their skills and knowledge, leading to improved outcomes in their work. Additionally, collaborating with leaders provides networking opportunities, allowing individuals to build connections and expand their professional network. These connections can open doors to new opportunities and resources that can further contribute to achieving better outcomes. P4 believes that by leveraging the collaborative relationship with leaders, individuals can maximize their potential and drive positive results in their work. P7 eloquently described the collaborative process within their company, wherein ideas and input seamlessly cascade from employees to managers and higher-level directors. This concerted approach nurtures cooperation and fosters a harmonious interaction across all organizational tiers, resulting in beneficial outcomes. The participant emphasized the importance of collaboration at every level, highlighting its significance in promoting teamwork and collective success. P8 also emphasized the importance of collaboration between teams and leaders, highlighting how when they work together, combining their expertise and aligning their actions with the company's vision, it creates a collaborative process that contributes to overall success. This collaboration allows for the effective execution of tasks and helps everyone in the organization thrive. P10 strongly believed in the connection between effective collaboration and the quality of outcomes, emphasizing that having the best leaders and collaborators working together on a project leads to high-quality results. Conversely, ineffective communication and inspirational leadership can result in incomplete or flawed outcomes.

Table 10

Collaboration and effective leadership, according to Theme 6

Codes	Category	Theme
Leadership		
Effective	Effective Leadership	
Collaboration		Collaboration and effective leadership
Stability		
Coalition		

Theme 6: Collaboration and Effective Leadership

The sixth theme, collaboration and effective leadership was derived from the Effective Leadership categories. Selecting theme six was relevant and aligned with research question two on the influence of collaborations between leaders and followers on employee satisfaction. This theme focused on understanding how effective leadership, particularly in fostering collaborative relationships, influences employee satisfaction within a banking context. The theme allowed the researcher to examine various aspects of effective leadership in fostering collaboration, such as communication, leadership, shared decision-making, and organizational stability. It provided an opportunity to explore how leaders create a collaborative work environment where employees feel valued, heard, and empowered to contribute their ideas and perspectives. The theme comprised five codes: leadership, effective, collaboration, stability, and coalition. This concept describes the connection between collaboration and effective leadership.

Collaboration was disclosed as a significant factor in determining effective leadership by the participants, and competent leaders can collaborate more effectively with their followers.

According to P2, a close relationship exists between collaboration and effective leadership. P2 recognizes that effective leaders understand the importance of collaboration in achieving organizational goals and fostering a productive work environment. They stated,

> I do believe that a correlation exists. I believe that in order to be an effective leader, one must be a team player. I believe you must be able to interact with a variety of people and be willing to listen to and consider ideas other than your own.

P2 believes leaders who actively promote and encourage collaboration among team members create an atmosphere where individuals can work together synergistically, leveraging their diverse skills and perspectives. P2 emphasizes that effective leaders facilitate open communication, promote teamwork, and create opportunities for flourishing collaboration. By fostering a collaborative culture, leaders empower their team members to share ideas, contribute their expertise, and work collectively towards common objectives. P2 firmly believes that when leaders prioritize and facilitate collaboration, it leads to more effective decision-making, innovative problem-solving, and overall better outcomes for the organization.

The fact that all participants in the focus groups shared the same viewpoint indicates a high degree of consensus regarding the relationship between collaboration and effective leadership. Collaboration can result in enhanced performance, improved team dynamics, and explicit communication, all essential for effective leadership. F2 stated, "I believe there is a direct relationship. I believe it will never be if you work for someone who is not a collaborator or with individuals who do not wish to collaborate. You will never be able to complete the task at the utmost level. I mean, it depends on the position, but I believe the relationship in a department is certainly'. F6 also stated,

> If you don't communicate your ideas, you won't receive any additional ones. You keep your notions to yourself, even though they are all useless. Do you get my meaning? For them to have a relationship with you, however, and for you to be an effective leader, you must be a competent collaborator.

According to P3, when there is a lack of collaboration, both parties involved are likely to experience a decrease in effectiveness. On the other hand, when collaboration is high, the effectiveness of both parties tends to increase significantly. P3 understands that effective collaboration enables individuals to work together more efficiently, leveraging each other's strengths and achieving shared goals more effectively. He emphasizes that collaboration enhances the overall effectiveness of individuals and teams by promoting open communication, knowledge sharing, and mutual support. P3 believes that when individuals collaborate effectively, they can tap into a collective pool of ideas, perspectives, and resources, leading to improved decision-making, problem-solving, and overall performance. Thus, P3 acknowledges the strong positive relationship between collaboration and effectiveness in achieving desired outcomes. Furthermore, P7 emphasizes the strong relationship between collaboration and career advancement within the bank, stating that individuals cannot progress within the organization without communication and collaboration. This underscores the importance of collaboration as a valued skill and a key factor in professional growth and development.

According to P10, collaboration is an essential aspect of effective leadership. P10 believes that leaders should actively engage in collaboration with their internal team, superiors, and subordinates. He emphasizes that collaboration acts as the glue that brings all parties together, fostering a cohesive and synergistic work environment. P10 recognizes that effective leaders understand the importance of working collaboratively to achieve common goals and drive success. By collaborating with team members, superiors, and subordinates, leaders can build strong relationships, facilitate open communication, and promote a culture of trust and mutual support. P10 suggests that without collaboration, there is a risk of fragmentation and lack of cohesion, which can hinder progress and impede the achievement of desired outcomes.
Therefore, P10 firmly believes that effective leaders should embrace collaboration as a key principle to foster teamwork, maximize collective potential, and drive positive results.

P11 further reinforces the link between collaboration and effective leadership. They explained that being a transformational leader involves sharing a vision with employees and gaining their buy-in through collaboration. Collaboration helps build trust between leaders and team members, fostering a positive work environment and facilitating the achievement of shared objectives. P13 highlights the role of leadership in encouraging collaboration. He noted that leadership direction plays a significant role in promoting collaboration among employees. When leaders actively encourage and support collaboration, it creates an enthusiastic environment where individuals work together towards long-term goals.

Summary

In this study, two research questions were addressed. To investigate these questions, the researcher utilized a qualitative descriptive study and conducted a thematic analysis to analyze and interpret the data. Through this process, six themes emerged from the coded data, providing insights and answers to the research questions. The six themes uncovered through this research are as follows:

Theme 1: Transformational leadership enhances performance
Theme 2: Transformational leadership influences employee loyalty
Theme 3: Transformational leadership result to desired outcome
Theme 4: Collaboration and employees' satisfaction
Theme 5: Collaboration and best results
Theme 6: Collaboration and effective leadership

The analysis of theme one revealed that inspiring and motivating employees to achieve their full potential and work toward a common goal improves the performance of bank employees. This is accomplished through the leader's ability to stimulate creativity, innovation, commitment, and loyalty. The analysis further demonstrated how transformational leadership positively impacts the performance of bank employees by increasing their motivation. This is achieved by providing a clear vision, inspiring them to work toward that vision, developing their skills and abilities, fostering a culture of innovation and creativity, and encouraging them to take responsibility for their work.

Transformational leadership has significantly impacted the bank's shared vision and predetermined objectives. These leaders inspire and motivate followers by aligning individual goals with organizational objectives, fostering commitment, engagement, and teamwork. They communicate the organization's vision and values effectively, ensuring everyone pursues the same objectives. Additionally, they generate urgency and significance around the vision, motivating employees to take action. Through this approach, transformational leaders provide purpose and meaning in work, enhancing job satisfaction and motivation. Establishing a shared vision and aligning individual goals with the organization's objectives can ultimately increase employee engagement, commitment, and motivation, leading to improved job performance and organizational outcomes.

The analysis of the second theme demonstrates that transformational leadership significantly impacts employee loyalty in the banking sector. These leaders are known for their ability to inspire and motivate their followers, instilling commitment and engagement. This, in turn, cultivates loyalty and commitment to the organization, leading to higher employee retention and reduced turnover rates. Through inspiring and motivating their followers, fostering commitment and engagement, providing support and recognition, and promoting a culture of learning and growth, transformational leaders enhance employee satisfaction, organizational performance, and create a positive work environment, ultimately fostering greater employee loyalty.

The analysis of Theme 3 demonstrates the significant impact of transformational leadership on desired outcomes. These leaders inspire and motivate their followers to pursue a shared vision, fostering alignment between individual goals and organizational objectives. As a result, transformational leaders cultivate employee commitment, engagement, and collaboration, enhancing job satisfaction and organizational performance. The analysis of Theme 3 further emphasizes the substantial influence of transformational leadership on banks' desired outcomes. These leaders communicate the organization's vision and values effectively, ensuring all employees are aligned with the same objectives.

The analysis of theme 4 suggested that collaboration is a significant factor in determining employee satisfaction. Collaboration is crucial in the banking industry because banks are complex organizations requiring employees with diverse skills and knowledge to achieve the desired result. Through collaboration, employees can learn from one another and acquire new skills, enhancing job performance and satisfaction. When employees collaborate, they develop relationships and connections with their coworkers, fostering social support and belonging at work. This can increase job satisfaction because employees will feel connected to their coworkers and the organization.

Also, collaboration between leaders and followers improves the performance of followers. Collaboration between leaders and followers entails working toward a shared objective, exchanging information, and establishing an open and transparent communication channel. When leaders collaborate effectively with their followers, they create a positive work environment that encourages collaboration, trust, and respect, enhancing their followers' performance.

The analysis of theme 5 showed that banks achieve optimal results through effective collaboration between leaders and followers. This cooperation necessitates joint efforts towards a shared goal, information exchange, and establishing an open and honest communication channel. A leader who effectively collaborates with their followers cultivates a positive work environment that encourages collaboration, trust, and respect. This, in turn, leads to the best outcomes for banks.

Upon analyzing theme 6, it was discovered that effective leadership and collaboration in the financial industry have a positive relationship. According to the findings, Leaders who collaborate with their followers tend to be more effective in their duties. These leaders communicate openly with their team members, establish shared goals and objectives, and encourage everyone to contribute ideas and insights toward attaining these goals. In addition, effective leadership and collaboration go hand in hand because they complement and reinforce one another. Leaders who collaborate effectively with their followers cultivate a cooperative and trustworthy work environment. This makes team members feel appreciated and empowered, increasing motivation, productivity, and improved outcomes. Effective collaboration has become a crucial leadership talent that can help organizations achieve their objectives and remain competitive. Therefore, executives need to recognize the importance of collaboration and foster a collaborative culture within their teams.

Conclusion

It can be concluded from the analysis that transformational leadership significantly impacts bankers' job satisfaction in the United States. Transformational leaders inspire their adherents to transcend self-interest and achieve a common objective. They encourage followers to realize their maximum potential by promoting shared visions and values. Transformational leaders also provide their adherents with support, recognition, and feedback, which can positively affect their job satisfaction. Transformational leaders are renowned for their ability to foster a gratifying and motivating work environment. They encourage open communication, teamwork, and trust, which can lead to greater job satisfaction. Transformational leaders can increase employee engagement and commitment by imbuing their employees' work with a sense of purpose and significance. In addition, transformational leaders foster a learning and growth culture in which employees are encouraged to take risks, learn from their mistakes, and develop continuously. Job satisfaction can increase when employees feel challenged and supported in their professional development.

Furthermore, collaborations between leaders and followers significantly impact employee satisfaction. Employees feel more engaged and motivated when leaders and followers collaborate to accomplish a common objective. Such collaborations can produce a positive work environment, improved communication, and a sense of trust between leaders and followers.

When leaders include their followers in decision-making, job satisfaction increases because employees feel valued and have a sense of ownership over their work. Collaboration also encourages creativity and innovation, enabling employees to generate new ideas and solutions, which can increase their job satisfaction. When leaders and followers collaborate, a sense of belonging and collaboration is created, which can positively affect employee morale. As employees become more invested in the organization's success, such collaborations can improve performance and productivity. Collaborations between leaders and subordinates are essential to employee contentment. By collaborating, leaders and followers can create a positive work environment, improve communication and trust, encourage creativity and innovation, and cultivate a sense of belonging and teamwork, resulting in greater job satisfaction and improved overall performance.

Chapter 5: Summary, Conclusions, and Recommendations

Introduction and Summary of Study

This study investigated the effect of transformational leadership on job satisfaction in the United States banking sector and it also examined the influence of collaborations between the leaders and followers on employees' satisfaction in the United States banking sector. To achieve this, the researcher utilized a qualitative descriptive research approach, conducting interviews and focus group discussions with 25 participants based on Zoom video teleconferencing. Fifteen out of the sampled participants were subjected to interviews while the remaining 10 participants were subjected to focus group discussions. The participants that constituted the focus group discussions were not part of the interview group. The participants used in this study were screened based on the following inclusion criteria of this study: a minimum of ten years working experience in the banking sector, a minimum of Associate degree/Bachelor of Science or Bachelor of Arts and an age range of 30 to 45 years (Appendix A).

The two research questions were answered in the study by analyzing the data collected from participants and presented the results based on findings of the analysis:

RQ1: How do bank employees describe the impact of transformational leadership on their job satisfaction?

RQ2: How do bank employees describe the influence of collaboration between the leaders and followers on employee satisfaction?

The collected data were transcribed, processed, and coded using MaxQDA version 12. The researchers identified various codes and merged them into categories, which were then further consolidated into nine themes that were analyzed. In this chapter, the study's results were summarized, conclusions were drawn from the summary of findings, the study's findings are discussed in relation to the analysis of data and recommendations are made for professionals and researchers based on the findings of the study, and suggestions are also made for future research.

Summary of Findings and Conclusion

The study findings indicated that motivating and inspiring bank employees to attain their highest potential and work towards a shared objective contributes to employee satisfaction and job satisfaction. The study noted that this satisfaction is associated with a leader's capacity to encourage creativity and innovation while nurturing a sense of dedication and loyalty among employees. Findings from the six themes analyzed in this study are summarized below.

Theme 1: Transformational Leadership and Performance: This theme explains how transformational leadership influences the performance of banking employees in the United States. Majority of participants emphasized that transformational leadership involves effective leadership and coaching and mentoring to enhance employee performance. This invariably have a positive effect on the overall performance of the organization. Most of the participants also emphasized that transformational leadership lead employees in the right way as well as coaching and mentoring of employees to improve employees' performance which invariably positively impact the organizational performance as a whole.

Theme 1 also revealed that transformational leadership provides the training necessary to comprehend and learn how to drive business, thereby positively influencing the bank's shared vision. It was submitted that when employees receive training and development opportunities, they are better able to comprehend the bank's goals and objectives, as well as how to accomplish them. This increase productivity, enhance performance, and creates a more committed workforce.

Transformational leadership improve team morale, productivity, and performance. By developing coaching skills, individuals are better guided and support their team members, leading to better outcomes for the organization. Furthermore, feeling trusted with tasks increases individual's sense of responsibility and accountability, motivating them to perform to the best of their abilities. The findings of theme 1 are consistent with Kalsoom et al. (2018) who stated that transformational leadership is a critical managerial quality that significantly impacts organizational performance and success. They also found that transformational leaders establish strong relationships with their followers to motivate, empower, and inspire them to achieve higher levels of performance.

Theme 2: Transformational Leadership Influence Employees' Loyalty: This theme explains the impact transformational leadership on employees' loyalty. The less likely an employee is to abandon a job, the greater his or her loyalty to the job. Participants disclosed that when employees are comfortable with the bank's leadership style, they do not consider changing jobs. The creation of a supportive work environment, the provision of opportunities for growth and development, and the fostering of a sense of shared purpose by transformational leaders can strengthen employees' connection to the organization and their intention to remain. The research suggests that when employees experience a sense of satisfaction stemming from the transformative leadership style of their superiors, they are more inclined to demonstrate loyalty towards their organization.

This result is in agreement with the job characteristics model, which argues that employee satisfaction is achieved through exposure to diverse tasks and the significance of their duties (George & Akinwale, 2020). The model opines that employees are more likely to feel a sense of fulfillment and enjoyment from their work when they have the opportunity to perform a range of different tasks and when they can see the importance and impact of their work on the broader organization or society (George & Akinwale, 2020). The model identifies five key job characteristics that are believed to lead to higher levels of employee motivation and satisfaction as skill variety, task identity, task significance, autonomy, and feedback.

The result is also evident from Ntayi et al., (2019), who suggested that creating a stable environment to develop employees is crucial in promoting their self-actualization needs. This requires a leader to exhibit emotional intelligence by aligning individual needs of followers to that of the organization. This finding is consistent with that of Seljemo et al. (2020), who found that transformational leadership styles positively influence employee satisfaction, work engagement, and psychosocial work environment while reducing adversity in the workplace. Similarly, Pateczek et al. (2018) suggested that transformational leaders enhance the satisfaction levels of their followers by impacting on their loyalty. This result of theme 3 is in alignment with the assertion of Bathena, (2018) who found that employees who are satisfied with their jobs tend to be more loyal to the company and its objectives and go extra mile to achieve a wide organizational goal. He further asserted that job satisfaction plays a crucial role in promoting employee loyalty towards the company and its objectives.

Theme 3: Transformational Leadership Results to Desired Outcome:

This theme emphasized the impact transformational leadership has on achieving the desired outcome.

Participants emphasized that transformational leadership positively affects the bank's intended outcome. They maintained that transformational leadership helps to achieve the intended outcome by continuously evaluating and reviewing employees' performance thereby encouraging regular communication between employees and their superiors in order to maintain clarity regarding goals, objectives, and expectations, as well as to resolve any issues or challenges that may arise during the course of work.

Theme 4: Collaboration and Employees' Satisfaction: This theme showed the influence of collaboration on employees' satisfaction. Participants revealed that collaboration between the leader and the adherents increases employee motivation and satisfaction. It was emphasized that when employees are encouraged to collaborate and share ideas, they perceive that their contributions are valued by their coworkers and the organization as a whole. This sense of recognition and appreciation can be a potent motivator for employees, fostering a sense of dedication and loyalty to the organization. The results of theme 4 of the study aligned with the conclusions of Salas-Vallina (2020), who found that effective collaboration between leaders and followers can bring several benefits to individuals and organizations, including employee satisfaction. By employing transformational leadership and collaboration, banks can create a more positive and productive work environment, where employees feel valued and supported, and are motivated to achieve their full potential. This can lead to increased job satisfaction, higher levels of performance, and ultimately, greater success for the organization as a whole.

Theme 5: Collaboration and Best Results: Theme 5 underscores the pivotal role of collaboration in achieving optimal results. Participants widely acknowledge that collaboration involves cooperation and synergy between leaders and followers, leading to the best possible outcomes. The theme revealed that collaboration encourages the free sharing of ideas and opinions, fostering an environment where individuals feel empowered to contribute their unique perspectives. The open exchange of ideas sparks enthusiasm and interest in the work, motivating employees to strive for excellence. Theme 5 highlights that collaboration serves as a catalyst for achieving optimal results. It empowers individuals to share ideas, learn from leaders, and work collectively towards excellence. The engagement of both employees and leaders in a collaborative process is shown to be fundamental to success in achieving the best possible outcomes.

Theme 6: Collaboration and Effective Leadership: Theme 6 described the connection between collaboration and effective leadership. Collaboration was disclosed to be a significant factor in determining effective leadership by the participants. They maintained that a competent leader will be able to collaborate with the followers more effectively. The participants believed there is a close relationship between collaboration and effective leadership. A collaborative environment that fosters innovation, engagement, and enhanced performance can be created by leaders who are receptive and willing to listen to their followers. Majority of the participants also believed that, in a collaborative setting, clear communication and feedback are also essential components of effective leadership.

Implications for the Study

The findings of this study have some implications for research and practice. The outcomes of this study have significant implications for the top management of banking institutions. The study suggested that adopting a transformational leadership approach could potentially enhance job satisfaction amongst bank employees. Therefore, the upper management of banks can take this finding as an opportunity to adopt transformational leadership techniques to improve employee morale, performance, and job satisfaction. By implementing transformational leadership style, managers can create a positive work environment where employees feel motivated to work towards achieving the organizational goals. This can lead to increased productivity, reduced absenteeism, and a higher rate of employee retention. As a result, organizations can benefit from a more satisfied and dedicated workforce, ultimately leading to the success of the organization.

The findings of this study hold practical implications for other industries and business owners. By understanding the effectiveness of transformational leadership, they can adopt this leadership style to achieve better outcomes for their organizations. Transformational leadership can improve employees' job satisfaction, which can lead to increased productivity and reduced employee turnover. Therefore, business owners can use the knowledge gained from transformational leadership to create a work environment that fosters employee satisfaction, which in turn, benefits the organization as a whole. Additionally, organizations can invest in training programs to develop their managers' transformational leadership skills, which can lead to a more engaged and motivated workforce.

The findings of this study also provided valuable insights for researchers who wish to delve into the connection between transformational leadership and the satisfaction of employees. These researchers will be able to build on the current study's methodology and results, as well as expand the scope of the research to include additional variables or samples. The study served as a road map for future research on the impact of transformational leadership on employees' satisfaction in the banking sector, potentially leading to more comprehensive and accurate findings.

Limitations of the study

This study has some limitations that were unavoidable due to constraints in time and resources. It is important to acknowledge these limitations and provide recommendations for future research. This research being a qualitative study, while valuable in exploring the intricacies and nuances of the research topic, has inherent limitations due to the inability to establish causal relationships between the variables of interest, which involve demonstrating a cause-and-effect connection between the dependent variable (employees' satisfaction) and independent variables (transformational leadership). This is difficult to establish in qualitative research designs.

In addition to the previously mentioned limitations, another significant concern in research is the potential influence of the researcher on the overall experience and the subsequent comprehension of the data collected. This issue arises from the inherent biases and subjectivity that researchers may bring to the study, which can affect the objectivity and accuracy of the findings. To mitigate this limitation, the researcher employed reflexivity, which involves self- awareness and critical reflection on the part of the researcher. Reflexivity allows researchers to recognize and acknowledge their own biases, assumptions, and preconceptions that might influence the research process and data interpretation (Clancy, 2013).

The utilization of purposive sampling technique was adopted in this study. However, it is important to acknowledge the limitations associated with this approach, as it involves a deliberate selection process that can result in the exclusion of various potential experiences (Emerson, 2015; Gyarmathy et al., 2014). Consequently, this limitation restricts the research by potentially overlooking significant and impactful experiences that could offer novel information and data beyond what is present in the selected sample of participants.

The employment of semi-structured questions during the interview and focus group discussion introduced a constraint on the participant's narrative direction (Cronin, 2014). As a result, there is a possibility of losing out on valuable experiences shared by the participants that could have emerged organically if the discussion had not been guided by the researcher.

The selection of participants from the same geographical location poses a limitation on the transferability of findings (Emerson, 2015; Gyarmathy et al., 2014). In qualitative case study designs, transferability relies on the emergence of themes and principles from participant narratives rather than the statistical data used in quantitative studies (Anderson et al., 2014). However, it is important to note that themes derived from participants in different geographical regions may not necessarily align, thus constraining the generalizability of the findings (Kandola, et. al, 2014). The study was focused on the banking sector and could have included a comparative analysis with other industries. However, due to limitations in time and resources, it was not possible to extend the scope of the research beyond the banking industry.

Suggestions for Future Research

This study examined the effect transformational leadership on employees' satisfaction in the United States banking sector. In order to gain a broader understanding of the impact of transformational leadership across different industries, future research should replicate the same research design with different population clusters such as the telecommunications industry, construction industry, hospitality industry, or even the manufacturing industry. By doing so, researchers can investigate if the same results can be found across different industries, and whether there are any industry-specific differences that need to be considered when implementing transformational leadership. This would enable organizations to have a better understanding of the best leadership practices and how they can be adapted to different industries for optimal results.

A potential avenue for future research could be a comparative study between the banking sector and other industries, to investigate the similarities and differences in the impact of transformational leadership on employees' satisfaction and organizational outcomes. This could provide insights into whether the findings of this study are specific to the banking sector or whether they can be generalized to other industries. Furthermore, such a study could provide useful information for managers and leaders in other industries who are interested in implementing transformational leadership practices to improve employee performance and organizational outcomes. A comparative study would require a larger sample size to ensure sufficient representation of the different industries and would also require careful selection of appropriate industries for comparison.

Using a quantitative research method for future studies would allow for the use of statistical analysis to test the significance of relationships between variables. This method would also allow for the use of a larger sample size, which would contribute to a more comprehensive understanding of the research. The use of surveys or questionnaires would be appropriate for collecting data in a quantitative study, as it would allow for the collection of large amounts of data from a wide range of participants. The results of a quantitative study would provide more precise and measurable findings that could be generalized to a larger population. Therefore, future researchers should consider using a quantitative research method to further investigate the relationship between transformational leadership and employee satisfaction in the banking sector.

www.ingramcontent.com/pod-product-compliance
Lightning Source LLC
LaVergne TN
LVHW011948070526
838202LV00054B/4845